MAKING the BEST of ME

A handbook for student excellence and self-esteem

TEACHER'S GUIDE | SECONDARY EDITION

Stu Semigran & Sindy Wilkinson

ACKNOWLEDGMENTS

OUR THANKS TO:

- John-Roger and John Morton for their on-going love and support.
- David Bransky, David Raynr, Patti Rayner, Marla Ludwig, Michael Hubbard, Deborah Turner-Bartholomew and the entire Insight and EduCare staffs for sharing the vision.
- Bruce Fox for his excellent art and design editing.
- Marsha Winborn for her talented work on illustrations.
- Connie Stomper and Bunny McLean for their contribution to the classroom activities.
- Margalit Finger-Ward, John Ward and the staff of Fingerprint Desktop Publishers for their assistance.
- Many outstanding leaders in the field of self-esteem education who have served as sources of inspiration for the concepts and activities in the workbook. Special thanks in particular to Candy Semigran, Russell Bishop, Lon Luty, Jack Canfield, John Vasconcellos, Robert Reasoner, Cliff Durfee, Peter McWilliams, Kathleen Carroll, Sandy Lynne, John Deanshaw, and Alec O'Halloran.
- Penelope Towle, Carol Towle, Gillian McNeese, Olga Messina, Holly Duggan, Margaret Peake, Given Eaton, Dee Dee Diemer, Diane Coogias, Michael McCarthy, Greg Hauca, Shar Kanan, Eisha Mason, and Berdel Warrior for their countless hours of devoted production assistance.
- Esther Jantzen and Lois Palio of Dobbins Vocational Technical High School, Philadelphia, PA, for their inspiration.
- Drs. John Whitaker, Grace Joely Beatty, and David Gardner for their assistance on research and evaluation of our EduCare Program.
- Our wonderful spouses, Candy Semigran and David Wilkinson, for their love, companionship, and tremendous support.

ADDITIONAL ACKNOWLEDGEMENT (June 2020)

- Armando Diaz, EduCare's Program Director, for guiding EduCare's virtual and digital webinars, virtual trainings, and digitizing the *Making the Best of Me* handbook.
- LaNell Williams, CEO at Athgo and EduCare facilitator, for skillfully coordinating EduCare's *Making the Best of Me* digitizing project team.
- Amy Bransky, Katherine Hall, Jim Levy, and Hillary Neumeister, and Julia Pepper for their thorough work on proofreading and editing.
- Eldrick Bone, Janvie Cason, Bryn Drescher, Eliana Farias, Raul Fernandez, Victoria Lantry, Yesenia Leon, Phil Ramirez, Rafael Romo, Jennie Rosenbaum, Frank Vitale, Margalit Ward, ACE Program facilitators & staff, and educators over the years for making these programs come alive for so many students.
- Colin Brooks, EduCare's Logistics and Supplies Coordinator, for his terrific assistance with the photographs.
- Laurel Brunson, graphic designer, who generously offered her talent and artistry to lead us in digitizing *Making the Best of Me*. We so appreciate her dedication and willingness to serve and for her tremendous work in redesigning the handbook in such an attractive and accessible style. We thank the Annenberg Foundation and Catchafire for introducing Laurel to EduCare.
- The educators, parents, and community partners, EduCare staff and board members for their amazing commitment each day in lifting the lives of thousands of deserving young people.

A SPECIAL THANKS

A special thanks to Patric Peake for his contribution to Chapter 7: Personal Journal. For many years, Pat was the principal of Aurora High School in Calexico, California. Aurora High School received numerous achievement awards, including the California School Board's "Golden Bell Award" for innovative education. In addition to creating a culture of kindness and compassion while at Aurora High School, Pat was a highly regarded storyteller and author. His book, *A Blink in the Eye of the Great Blue Heron* depicts inspiring and heartfelt stories of his students. We are deeply grateful to Pat for his enduring contribution to the lives of so many students whose lives he helped shape.

CONTENTS

vii   Introduction for Teachers
xvi   Introduction *(from Student's Handbook)*

1 GETTING TO KNOW EACH OTHER

I-04	Friendship Pie
I-06	Autobiographical Sketch
I-12	Match Up Game
I-14	Cooperative Games
I-20	Class Contract
I-22	Landmarks in my Life
I-24	Getting to Know Someone
I-26	Meet Someone Unique
I-27	Map Autobiography
I-28	Learning Chain
I-29	Photo Search
I-30	Free Advice
I-31	Mystery Person
I-32	If You Only Knew
I-33	Secret Buddy
I-34	Grab Bag
I-35	Hot Seat
I-36	Speaking Out
I-38	Castles in the Class
I-39	Great Person of the Year

2 BUILDING SELF-ESTEEM

II-04	Appreciation
II-06	Be a Friend to Yourself
II-08	Positive Qualities
II-10	Good News
II-12	Bragging
II-14	Unstructured Writing

II-16	Admiration Mirror
II-18	Self-Talk
II-22	Putdowns
II-24	Letting Go
II-28	Keeping Track of Negative Self-Talk
II-29	Practicing Positive Self-Talk
II-32	Self-Forgiveness
II-34	Positive Feedback Cards
II-35	Acknowledgment
II-36	Affirmations
II-40	Student Affirmation
II-42	Advertising Me
II-44	Come On Down
II-46	I Am Grateful For
II-48	Gratitude
II-50	Super Me Cape
II-52	Letter to Yourself
II-54	Super Booster

3 CREATING POSITIVE RELATIONSHIPS

III-04	Making Friends
III-06	Power of Friendships
III-10	Friendship
III-12	What's My Feeling?
III-13	Keeping Friends
III-14	Trusting
III-16	The Ties That Bind
III-18	Team Tale
III-20	Telephone
III-22	I'm Listening
III-24	What I Heard You Say Was...
III-26	Point of View
III-28	Talking It Out: Resolving Conflict
III-30	Trust Circles
III-32	Expressing Resentments and Appreciations
III-34	Heart-Seat
III-35	Brainstorming
III-38	Tell it to the Teacher
III-39	Button Pushing
III-40	Forgiving
III-42	Coaching Partners
III-44	Survival
III-48	Making a Difference in Someone's Life

4 PERSONAL RESPONSE-ABILITY

IV-04	Caring for Yourself
IV-06	Taking Care of Yourself and Helping Others
IV-08	Games People Play
IV-10	Examining Attitudes
IV-14	Have To/Choose To
IV-16	Impossible? Maybe Not!
IV-18	Changing Attitudes
IV-22	Learning from Mistakes
IV-24	Mock Argument
IV-26	Are Your Feelings Driving You?
IV-30	Letting Go of Judgment and Guilt
IV-34	Letting Go of Resentment
IV-38	Risk Exercise
IV-40	I Scare Myself
IV-42	Meet the Press
IV-44	Take a Stand
IV-46	I Agree/I Disagree
IV-47	Can I Quote You on That?
IV-48	Viewpoints in the Round
IV-50	Broken Agreements
IV-54	Taking Charge

5 ACHIEVING EXCELLENCE

V-04	Getting What You Want
V-06	A New Reality
V-10	Why Go to School Anyway?
V-14	Dreaming
V-18	King/Queen of the World
V-20	Creating the New Year
V-26	The Successes of My Life
V-28	From Limitation Into Expansion
V-32	The Data Dump
V-34	Cycle of Action
V-38	Magnificence
V-40	Creative Visualization
V-44	Ideal Scene
V-46	Mind Mapping
V-48	Goal Setting - Part 1 (Guidelines)
V-52	Goal Setting - Part 2 (Action Plan)
V-56	Daily Goals
V-58	Weekly Planner
V-62	Six Steps to Achieving Excellence
V-66	Managing Money
V-70	Treasure Maps
V-72	The Week in Review - 1
V-76	The Week in Review - 2

6 REACHING OUT TO YOUR FAMILY AND COMMUNITY

VI-04	Family Positions Everyone!
VI-05	Family Dynamics
VI-06	Heart to Heart
VI-08	Appreciation Letter
VI-10	Strength Circles
VI-12	What If I Were a Parent?
VI-14	Family Talk
VI-16	Letter of Acknowledgment
VI-18	Connecting with Family: Activities
VI-20	"Make My Day"
VI-22	Keys to Happiness
VI-24	What Can I Give?
VI-26	Making a Difference: Service

7 PERSONAL JOURNAL

VII-04	Teacher Journal Preparation
VII-06	Teacher Journal Work
VII-08	Guidelines for Reading Student Journals
VII-10	Student Journal Part 1
VII-11	Reflections
VII-16	Honesty Wheel
VII-20	Looking Back Over My Week
VII-22	Student Journal Part 2

A APPENDIXES

A-02	EduCare at a Glance
A-04	Bibliography
A-06	Activities Calendar
A-08	Index (alphabetical by exercise)
A-10	About the Authors

> *"Whether you think you can or you can't, you are probably right."*
> – Henry Ford

INTRODUCTION FOR TEACHERS

The gift and opportunity of being a teacher is a precious one. Amidst the consistent challenges that face an educator, the hope, the vision, and the initial dream of why you became a teacher often appears dim or even lost. For the vast majority of educators, there is a hope and a belief that through your wisdom, your sharing of yourself, and perhaps foremost your caring for young people, you can play a positive and meaningful part in their growth.

SELF-ESTEEM IS THE FOUNDATION.

Jerry was a bright, likable eighth grader with a delightfully impish sense of humor. Academically he was slightly below average, though he seemed to be a student who could easily achieve excellent grades. On the morning of a "test" day, Jerry meandered into class and stopped by my desk as he often did to say hello. He looked up, smiled a bit, and declared, "You know what, I am going to fail that test today."

I paused a second and looking directly at him, commented, "Yes, I bet you are."

He was startled. "What type of comment is that from my history teacher who is typically a really caring guy?" he may have thought.

"Jerry," I went on, "if you've already been telling yourself that you think you'll fail that's what you'll probably do."

Somewhere along the line, Jerry had learned to give up. He was like vast numbers of young people today, who are giving up on their education, their families, their futures, themselves, and their lives . . . and are turning to alcohol, drugs, sex, crime, or suicide.

To believe in a dream of building a joyful and rewarding life that is personally fulfilling and that contributes to others, a student needs to believe deeply from within that he/she is worthy and capable of such a dream. For if he/she does not believe in his/her intrinsic goodness and essential value, then the best of courses with the most advanced educational materials will fall short.

WHAT CAN WE DO?

As a rule, we care. We want the most for our students. As teachers, we may sometimes discover moments when "everything seems to be going right". Perhaps we don't really know how or why these positive moments occur. These are the moments when a class, a student, or a teacher is clearly demonstrating high self-esteem. The learning experience sparkles with aliveness and vitality. The reservoir of self-esteem becomes deeper and, in turn, serves as a solid foundation for future teachable moments.

We may realize that it is not enough to "catch" only a few of those "shining" moments when it is all worth it. Our students are too important. The reasons for devoting ourselves to teaching are too valuable and sincere. We personally deserve to have the satisfaction of making a difference in another's life and in experiencing our success.

Consciously creating a school or class environment that fosters self-esteem is essential. It can also be incredibly rewarding to teach in an environment of caring and support. The process may not always be easy, yet with a clear intention and creative methods, building self-esteem in the classroom can be a delight.

Numerous studies report that as the self-concept of a student is enhanced, academic achievement rises. The student who feels good about himself naturally excels.

THE ROLE OF THE TEACHER IN BUILDING SELF-ESTEEM

START WHERE YOU ARE

There may never be the best class, enough time, enough training, etc. Start from where you are. If you know the value of self-esteem building and are willing to be the "student" of how best to teach it, go forward. Be willing to make mistakes as you learn along the way.

As it's been said, "The journey of a thousand miles, begins with the first step." Step into and commit to enhancing self-esteem.

YOU MAKE A DIFFERENCE

Think back to those teachers who made a lasting impression on you, ten years ago, twenty years ago or longer. In each of our lives, there are special people who have made great contributions to our growth. We can hold that place and make that impact on our students.

"SUPERTEACHER"

Since you are one who can "change the course of a young person's life," you may think that means that you need to be perfect. How about being human, instead? Accept the times when you "blow it" and move on. Have you ever spent minutes dwelling on that one student that you "lost it with" rather than the thirty-some others with whom you did well? Accept your strengths, your weak spots, and learn from the experience. (Isn't that what you tell your students?) Be open to letting your students know you. As they experience you with your personal ups and downs and your honesty about it, they can be more secure in their own risking to express and relate more openly and honestly.

MODEL SELF-ESTEEM

Building your personal self-esteem is not only a self-enhancer but it is a necessity in bringing positive self-esteem more fully into the classroom. You are a model. Be willing to explore and grow in your self-development and share that part of yourself with your students. There is a misconception that unless we keep our distance, we will not be able to effectively establish discipline. What if the source of the most productive discipline is the respected and caring teacher?

SHOW YOUR CARING FOR YOUR STUDENTS BY CARING FOR YOURSELF

Being the martyr, the one who is so stressed because you "try so hard" does not work. It does not work for your students, and it certainly does not work for you. By physically, emotionally, mentally, and spiritually caring for yourself, you are, in fact, providing a great gift to your students. When you do, you naturally have more of you to give, and you're exemplifying high self-esteem.

ACCEPTANCE VS. THE MYTH OF THE PERFECT STUDENT

Somewhere off on a distant planet (or classroom) there just may be some perfect students. They just never seem to show up in your room. Just as there are no perfect teachers, there are no perfect students. Acceptance works wonders, especially acceptance without conditions attached. What if each student is truly "lovable and capable" and that all of their behavior is really an attempt to meet certain needs in the best way they know? Perhaps each child is doing the best he/she possibly can with all that he/she has to work with (i.e., a troubled homelife, a low self-concept, a weak bladder, a rash of acne with the dance two nights away . . .).

The freer you are in accepting them, the easier it becomes for students to discover their own worthiness. Specifically, students need to know that rather than being ignored, discredited, or ridiculed, what they have to say will be accepted. Acceptance does not mean agreement. It is honoring each person's point of view as valuable.

Help yourself to a good dose of self-acceptance. This does not mean to dismiss standards you hold for yourself. It means you're human, as are your students; and, at times, you are going to do things in the classroom that you wish you hadn't. You might as well accept those, too. Life moves on, and with acceptance there is a lot more room for understanding, learning, and change.

STUDENTS DON'T CARE HOW MUCH YOU KNOW, UNTIL THEY KNOW HOW MUCH YOU CARE

Express your caring in the many ways you best know how. Through your sincere caring, students feel valued and important.

Greeting them, calling them by name, making eye contact, and sincerely listening to them lets them know that you respect them. You can be caring and still be the "adult." Also, encourage an atmosphere of mutual caring and appreciation.

Guide the class in routinely sharing compliments and expressions of support and acknowledgment directly with each other. Instead of sarcasm or looking to find fault in another, let everyone start trying to "catch each other being good or succeeding."

Learning accelerates when acceptance is present and caring is openly expressed.

WIN IN YOUR TEACHER FANTASY

"How can I ever teach THESE kids?"

"Look at him/her. There's no way that he/she will come around."

Assume the worst from your students and you'll probably get it. If you are going to fantasize about how your class will turn out (and you will), you might as well win in your fantasy. Enough has been documented about self-fulfilling prophecies to assist us in remembering that all students are capable of excellence. Prepare, expect, and challenge them to excel. Students can enjoy rising to meet the challenge as well as learning from the experience, if and when they may fall short. Expecting students to do well and teaching them to set clear and attainable goals allows them to "stretch into success". When little is expected of students, they develop self-concepts of believing they are not capable.

Success breeds self-esteem. Jaime Escalante, the acclaimed teacher from Garfield High School in Los Angeles (the subject of the inspiring movie, Stand and Deliver) states it simply in the motto that he repeatedly shares with his students; "You Can Do It! You Can Do It!" Believe in your students. It is a step in their believing in themselves.

CREATING A SUPPORTIVE AND AFFIRMING CLASSROOM ENVIRONMENT

Recall walking into a meeting or situation where the pervasive energy was tense and guarded. What would you rather have? How about a gathering of friends earnestly working on a project while sharing responsibility and warm feelings? Such an environment would generate:

- a sense of security
- a respect, appreciation, and caring of one another
- a feeling of belonging and inclusion
- an unconditional acceptance and support
- a foundation of trust
- a win-win cooperative attitude
- clear knowledge of expectations and goals
- joint decision-making opportunities and accountability for progress
- honest and caring communication
- a willingness to risk and to challenge oneself
- an upward spiral of success

It can easily be perceived that students come into "our" classes to learn the things that "we teach them." What if the classroom becomes a social environment that generates learning? The teacher is the master conductor, the facilitator ("facile"- to make easy) of the process rather than the spotlight attraction.

The creative, shared learning process becomes the focus. The class members mature as responsible co-creators by being guided towards and assuming greater ownership of their educational experience.

ABOUT THE PROGRAM

Making the Best of Me provides a comprehensive approach to positive self-esteem and life skills education for secondary level students. The program is divided into seven chapters:

1. Getting to Know Each Other
2. Building Self-Esteem
3. Creating Positive Relationships
4. Personal Response-Ability
5. Achieving Excellence
6. Reaching Out to Your Family and Community
7. Personal Journal

The chapters, for the most part, naturally build upon one another. Some of the activities from later chapters will be introduced early on and many of the group-building and self-esteem enhancers are excellent to weave in throughout. The Personal Journal section, though placed at the end of the handbook, is best introduced during the first two weeks of the term.

"Getting to Know Each Other" (Chapter 1) establishes a base of trust and mutual support for the class. Activities are designed so that students easily learn about one another, their commonality and uniqueness, as they naturally build an environment in which they can feel safe.

"Building Self-Esteem" (Chapter 2) lays a foundation for enhanced positive self-concept in practicing the skills for self-appreciation, acknowledgment, forgiveness, constructive self-talk, and affirmations.

"Creating Positive Relationships" (Chapter 3) explores the self-imposed barriers and enhancers to friendships. Activities focus on empathetic listening and communication skills. A cooperative team-building attitude resulting in the ability to build win-win relationships is strengthened.

"Personal Response-Ability" (Chapter 4) develops positive attitudes, decision making, and problem solving skills. The "blaming habit" is replaced by the freedom, clarity, and personal strength that results from being response-able to make choices that best serve oneself and others.

"Achieving Excellence" (Chapter 5) provides students with practical techniques for managing themselves, their school work, and their personal lives more productively. Through mind-mapping, visualizations, goal setting, and project planning , students gain expertise in creating self-motivating habits of achievement and success.

"Reaching Out To Our Families and Communities" (Chapter 6) allows students, through in-class and take home activities, to heal some of the misunderstanding and hurt that they may have with their families. Families are invited to participate at home in valuable and enjoyable communication, appreciation, and trust building activities. Students also experience them-selves as powerful contributors to their communities as they create ways to reach out in serving and giving to individuals and the community as a whole.

"Personal Journal" (Chapter 7) is a powerful vehicle for students to freely express their feelings and thoughts on a wide range of personal self-discovery topics.

HOW TO USE THE HANDBOOK

The handbook is primarily designed to be used as text for an on-going personal development, life-skills, human relations course.

More and more schools are understanding the need for and implementing self-esteem, life-skills development courses as a standard part of their required or elective courses.

Teachers, who are not teaching an ongoing personal development type course, can set aside regular 15 - 30 minutes blocks of time on a daily or weekly basis to present the activities in their standard classes. Starting early in the school year, choose activities that best meet your particular needs.

In addition, the handbook activities can be incorporated into existing subject matter. Interviews with historical figures, affirmations and visualizations as preparation for projects and tests, project planning, mind-mapping, treasure mapping, and many of the activities have direct application to subject material. The option notes on the activity instruction pages offer suggestions on how the activities can be applied to subject material. Rather than "taking time away" from the lesson at hand, the activities and learning approaches can often be the spark for renewed enthusiasm and participation in the subject at hand.

There are also many different cooperative learning approaches that are at the core of the activities which can used in most classes. They include team teaching, peer coaching, interview techniques, role-playing, brainstorming, and a variety of group involvement formats. Enjoy getting creative with what is here. There is a preview section at the beginning of each chapter that highlights each activity, its main focus, the time needed, and whether there is a student activity sheet for it. By familiarizing yourself with these previews, you can determine which activities to use.

Your teacher's edition also includes instructions for each of the various activities. The teacher activity instruction pages describe the purpose of the activity, the step by step procedure, suggestions for discussion, and options and tips on extending the activity further. The activities have been purposely sequenced within each chapter. Often, the concepts introduced later on in the chapter have been seeded earlier.

Thoroughly previewing the chapter ahead of time will allow you to know if making changes in the sequence might fit the particular needs or interests of your students.

Be aware that some of the activities, particularly in Chapter 5 ("Achieving Excellence"), may be slightly advanced for a typical seventh or eighth grade class.

The activities in Chapters 1 and 2 can be used well in conjunction with each other. As a safe environment gets established, through the development of class rules and group inclusion activities in Chapter 1, mixing in the self-esteem activities in Chapter 2 works excellently.

Also, Chapters 4 and 5 blend naturally together. Once there is a strong sense of personal responsibility as set forth in Chapter 4, learning activities from Chapter 5 can be introduced.

The activities from Chapter 6 that focus on reaching out to their families and the community can be introduced after the students have worked with the first two chapters. The "Personal Journal" (Chapter 7) is best to be introduced very early on, as mentioned previously, and worked with on a regular basis.

Feel free to adapt, modify, or expand upon the activities. It is fine to repeat certain favorite activities. Also, your class and you may find just the perfect way to mold a certain activity and make it yours. One activity may take your class off into an incredibly valuable tangent. (One ninth grade class got so involved with the role-playing activities for conflict resolution that they created a video/drama club to perform, film, and share their role-plays with other classes at the school.)

As you use the activities, allow the class to give you feedback as to what is and is not working. Take time regularly for open discussion and find ways to incorporate their improvement suggestions.

Have fun and allow yourself the joy of developing closer ties with your students. Take part in the activities and discussions actively yourself. Permit yourself to use your teaching of this material as your practice field for developing greater personal achievement and higher self-esteem.

Realize that the program is not meant to be a panacea. To produce individuals who are forever and always self-esteeming is unrealistic. Many factors, both present and past, play into the evolving of a student's self-concept. That is one of the reasons why the course not only involves the individual student but his/her teacher, peers, family, and community. There may be times over the course of a semester when it appears as if the class is backsliding. Relationships may seem to be deteriorating, motivation may be dropping or self-esteem may be wavering. That is natural.

Rather than using those moments/days to discredit progress that your students and you have made, take it as a signal that you may have hit some issues that individuals or the group are now ready to address. What if those moments are feedback, subtle indicators of what the students need more or less of to get back on track?

Know that these activities will bring up new awarenesses and feelings. Your students will be looking at themselves and their lives in ways that will create new insights and understanding.

Be patient with them and yourself. Do not expect a miracle overnight. For some students the growth can be more obvious and for others the course just may be laying the foundation for the possibility of an affirming self-image. These activities can be looked at as the exercise room or weight training for self-esteem and positive life skills. It takes time and practice for these "muscles" of confidence, trust, friendship, personal and social responsibility to develop. Enjoy the activities and the process through which you and your students can develop "muscles" which can last a lifetime.

INTRODUCTION FOR STUDENTS

Welcome to Making the Best of Me!

You deserve the best! You deserve the best not because of what you say (which isn't always the "best") or what you do (likewise). Just because you are alive, you deserve to experience the best . . . the best of friendships, the best in school, the best of jobs, the best with your families, the best in your future, and most importantly perhaps, the best of knowing and believing in yourself. The great thing about it is that you can have the best. You truly can. The catch is that it is up to you to do something about it.

Giving up is easy, and not having what you want in your life is easy. You can have all the greatest of reasons why life isn't the way you want. (i.e., "Life is a mess because it's THEIR fault. I'm too tired. It's boring. I don't have the money. They won't let me. My school/teacher/parent/brother/etc. get in the way."). These are great reasons and it's your life. With the reasons and without the reasons, it is still going to be your life. Make the very best of it . . . of you.

Did you know that Albert Einstein almost flunked out of high school? Winston Churchill was last in his class in school. Abraham Lincoln lost six different elections before he was finally elected as President. Despite the failures (and they too had all the perfect reasons for giving up), they all had one thing in common. It was a dream to have a fulfilling and rewarding life.

> *"There's nothing too good for you to possess,*
> *Nor heights where you cannot go.*
> *Your power is more than belief or guess,*
> *It's something you have to know.*
> *There's nothing to fear - you can and you will,*
> *For you're the invincible you.*
> *So set your foot on the highest hill,*
> *There's nothing you cannot do."*
>
> – Anonymous

<u>Making the Best of Me</u> is designed to give you the tools for making your life the way you'd like it to be. You will be able to learn ways to build more self-confidence, create the friendships you'd like, and achieve greater success in school. The handbook can make it easier for you to improve your relationship with your family, clarify and create more of what you want, and acquire skills for reaching your goals at school and in your personal life.

As you use the handbook, you can discover a lot about yourself. You can make new discoveries about who you are, what you want, and the ways you think and feel about things. The activities can be very special. Some of the ideas and approaches may be new to you. Try them out and get involved. You will see that it is up to YOU to get the most out of the handbook. As you write, discuss, and work with others on the activities, practice being honest with yourself and others. What if there really is no need to have to impress anyone?

A lot of the activities will involve working together with everyone in your class. Have you ever surprised yourself and made friends with someone you thought you'd never like? Be open to discover a lot of new friends in your class. You may find friends who have a lot of the same feelings that you do. As you are willing to support, respect, and appreciate one another, you can experience your class "coming together" and having lots of fun along the way.

Please let us know which chapters and activities you particularly liked or didn't like, and give us any ideas you have for improving them. We want to make the handbook the best, and appreciate your suggestions.

Realize that it is up to you to make your class and these activities something great! It is worth it. You are worth it!

CHAPTER 1
Getting to Know Each Other

TEACHING TIPS & SUGGESTIONS

1 Set up the activities with a blend of enthusiasm, encouragement, and patience. Group acceptance is of utmost importance to teens. The group inclusion activities are designed to let them easily "break the ice" and build trust within the group. It is okay to let them know that some of the activities (particularly the cooperative games) might at first seem silly or foolish. Encourage them to jump in and have fun.

2 Include yourself, as often as possible, in the games and group sharing activities. At times, go first and set the tone. Demonstrate taking risks and being vulnerable.

3 Let these activities be lighthearted and fun. There is no one best way for the activities to be done. Laughter is a great medicine. Be open for yourself and others to share a joke or a comical moment.

4 Come back to their favorite cooperative games (i.e., clump, hand squeeze, etc.) throughout the year. Use them especially when the class needs a physical or emotional boost. Have different students lead the interactive games at times.

5 Be a guide, coach, or facilitator. At times it may be wise to give up some of the need to control exactly how the activity is to unfold, and to let the spontaneity of the group take over. There is an art to permitting ample space for creativity to spark and letting an activity takes its own course without having the energy drop. Discovering this may take some practice and experience.
Be patient.

6 Form resource groups. Have students form set groups comprised of the same 5-7 students that will stay together for many of the small group activities throughout the term. These groups provide the students with an ongoing support base. Encourage a mix of people in each group- by gender, interest, and association. Advise students not to group with their best friends. Have them meet new people. It is suggested that the class divide into resource groups after some of the group activities have been introduced, and a sense of group trust and belonging has started to develop.

Many of the interview, name games, brainstorming, decision-making, group projects, and team-teaching activities work well in resource groups. Also set up random groupings at times, so students get to work with a variety of students. When the resource groups first meet, have them choose a group name and group cheer that they can use whenever they join together. Resource groupings can be changed every two or three months.

7 Clarify the class rules early on in the course. (See "Class Contract" for activity on setting up ground rules.) Students feel secure when they know the limits and what to expect. Having them take part in forming the rules develops trust and personal ownership. Discuss the value of the class having a confidentiality rule, so they can be assured that what they may share about themselves in the class will not be passed around the school. See that rules are consistently followed. If you are about to revise a norm, be clear in communicating the change.

8 Develop trust with the class by holding to the personal agreements and promises that you have made.

9 Be willing to deal with what's present. Use challenging situations that arise as opportunities for everyone to gain new insights. For instance, if a student is unusually sad or withdrawn, you may choose to move off the planned lesson and check in with the student. It may lead to an opportunity in which the whole group could offer encouragement and support. At other times, it may be wisest to, later on, privately check in with the student. Letting the students experience that you and the class, during difficult times, can be there for one another may prove to be a powerful experience.

10 Plan to introduce the Personal Journal (Chapter 7) work within the first two weeks of the term.

ACTIVITY PREVIEWS

FRIENDSHIP PIE
Focus: Fun, safe way to meet new friends through milling
Time: 15 minutes
Activity: Page I-05

AUTOBIOGRAPHICAL SKETCH
Focus: Self-introspection through questionnaire
Time: Varies
Activity: Page I-08

MATCH UP GAME
Focus: Learn about others in a non-threatening way
Time: 15 minutes
Activity: Page I-13

COOPERATIVE GAMES
Focus: Build group cohesiveness through fun, active games
Time: 10-15 minutes each

CLASS CONTRACT
Focus: Establish class rules and norms through group participation
Time: 50 minutes

LANDMARKS IN MY LIFE
Focus: Identify major changes that affected how we think and behave
Time: One week homework project
Activity: Page I-23

GETTING TO KNOW SOMEONE
Focus: Interview others
Time: One or two class periods
Activity: Page I-25

MEET SOMEONE UNIQUE
Focus: Meet new people and appreciate individual uniqueness through interviewing
Time: 30-40 minutes

MAP AUTOBIOGRAPHY
Focus: Artistically describe and share the major events in life
Time: 30-45 minutes

LEARNING CHAIN
Focus: Share personal interests; cooperative learning
Time: 20-30 minutes

PHOTO SEARCH
Focus: Become more comfortable in the group while having fun
Time: 10 minutes

FREE ADVICE
Focus: Share points of view in a non-threatening exercise
Time: 30 minutes

MYSTERY PERSON
Focus: Fun way to get to know classmates and build group cohesiveness
Time: 10 minutes

IF YOU ONLY KNEW
Focus: Low risk self-disclosure to build cohesion
Time: 20-30 minutes

SECRET BUDDY
Focus: Build caring relationships and experience the fun of giving and receiving
Time: 10 minutes

GRAB BAG
Focus: Build group trust and encourage personal sharing in a fun, safe way
Time: 20 minutes

HOT SEAT
Focus: Practice communication skills through sharing personal beliefs, feelings, and interests in small groups
Time: 15-30 minutes

SPEAKING OUT
Focus: Speak out and be listened to on important issues
Time: 20-30 minutes

CASTLES IN THE CLASS
Focus: Build group cooperation skills through non-verbal activity
Time: 20-30 minutes

GREAT PERSON OF THE YEAR
Focus: Build positive feelings
Time: 50 minutes

FRIENDSHIP PIE

PURPOSE

1. To experience meeting new friends in a fun, safe and accepting way.

2. To recognize the uniqueness of each of us as individuals.

PROCEDURE

Have students complete the activity sheet and then the milling process as outlined on the sheet.

DISCUSSION

1. How did you feel meeting one another? Was it easy or uncomfortable for you?

2. What did you learn about yourself? About others?

3. What did you learn about people in regards to the variety of answers to the questions?

FRIENDSHIP PIE

1. Place your name in the center of the wheel.

2. Write one answer in each section near the outer edge of the pie.

3. Mill around the room and initial each person's wedge that matches yours. Have them initial your wedge as well.

4. Find as many people as possible who match to initial your wedge, and you theirs. Have fun!

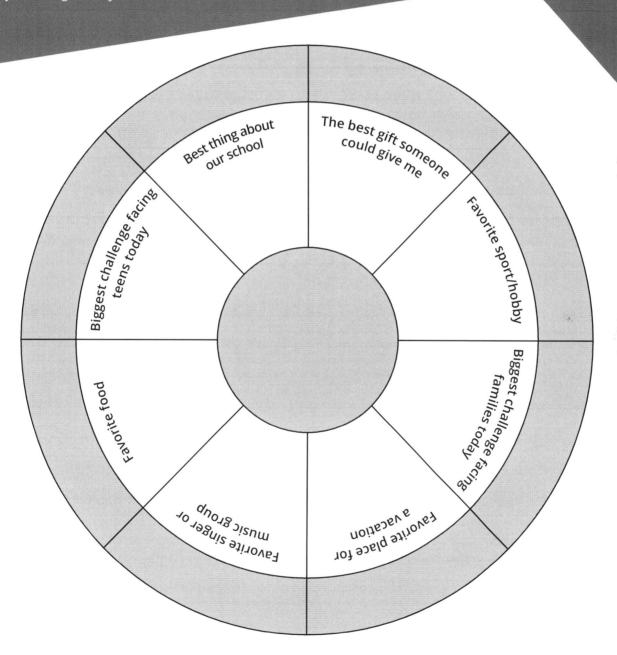

MAKING THE BEST OF ME | CHAPTER 1: I-05

AUTOBIOGRAPHICAL SKETCH

PURPOSE

1. Provide a tool for students to gain enhanced perspectives of themselves.

2. To encourage personal responsibility for activities and feelings.

PROCEDURE

1. Have students fill out the questionnaire carefully. Additional time at home may be required.

2. Without referring to the original questionnaire, have students complete a new form at the end of semester.

3. Stress individual responses and that there are no right or wrong answers.

4. After students complete the second questionnaire, have them compare it with the first one to note how their answers have changed or not.

DISCUSSION

In reviewing their beginning and end-of-the-year autobiographies, focus with the class on realizing that there are no "right" or "wrong" answers. Everyone's history and preferences are equally valuable. Lead a discussion on how the students feel about any changes they did or did not make. Explore how each one of us is responsible for (and therefore in control of) our feelings, changes and reactions.

AUTOBIOGRAPHICAL SKETCH

Fill out the questionnaire below. Take the time to consider each question carefully. You may discover some new things as you go along.

1. Name:

2. Birthdate:

3. Address and Phone:

4. Age:

5. List 10 words that describe you:

    1.   6.

    2.   7.

    3.   8.

    4.   9.

    5.   10.

6. What are your three best qualities?

    1.

    2.

    3.

7. List 5 words to describe each person in your family.

Would you show them this list?

8. How would you describe your relationship with your family?

What part do you play in creating this type of relationship?

9. What do you see yourself doing 5 years from now?

10 years?

20 years?

10. How do you spend your time after school and on weekends?

Is this how you want to spend your time?

11. Of all the things you do in your free time, which do you like the most?

The least?

12. What are the qualities (no names, please) of adults that you respect and admire most?

Do you have some of these qualities?

What are you doing to enhance them or develop them in yourself?

13. What are the qualities of adults you admire and respect the least?

Do you have some of these qualities?

What can you do to avoid developing these qualities in yourself?

14. Do you have any favorite sports, hobbies, or crafts? If so, what are they?

15. What are your favorite TV programs?

16. What magazines do you enjoy reading regularly, if any?

17. What about you makes you likable to your friends?

18. What major goals or objectives do you have right now?

What are you doing to accomplish them?

19. What does friendship and being a friend mean to you?

20. What do you think of school?

What changes would you like to see at your school?

21. Are you happy with yourself?

In what ways would you like to change, if any?

MATCH UP GAME

PURPOSE

1. To enhance group cohesiveness.

2. To discover commonalities amongst classmates.

PROCEDURE

1. Students write in their answers on the activity sheet.

2. Then, moving about, their task is to share their activity sheet with others and find at least one other student who matches up in each category. The "matched up" person writes their initials in the right column. More than one "matched up" person can initial the same category, and a person can initial more than one category.

DISCUSSION

1. Was it easy or difficult to find common experiences among your classmates?

2. Do you feel closer to the people in the class? If so, what brought that about?

MATCH UP GAME

NAME:

ITEM	MY ANSWER	OTHER PERSON'S INITIALS
Month of Birth		
Favorite T.V. Show		
Favorite Hobby		
Favorite Music Group		
Favorite Pet		
Number of Brothers		
Number of Sisters		
Favorite Food		
Favorite Number *(1 to 10)*		
Favorite Color		
Favorite Holiday		
Favorite School Subject		
Favorite Sport		
Favorite Movie Star		
I feel hurt when…		
I wish I had time to…		
I love…		

COOPERATIVE GAMES

PURPOSE

1. To develop and enhance group effectiveness and trust.

2. To have fun.

PROCEDURE

Each activity has a description of procedure. These games are wonderful icebreakers. Cooperative games are meant to be silly and playful. The group support and spirit takes the place of a need for winners and losers. You may want to move some desks and chairs to provide ample room for unobstructed movement. Enjoy the fun of these cooperative games!

* Thanks to The New Games Book and the Play Fair book from which several of these activities have been adapted. See the bibliography for more information.

NAME GAMES

These are fun and self-affirming games by which students learn each other's names.

1. The class sits in a circle and the first person says "I am Jim." The person to the right then says, "He is Jim and I am Fran." The person to their right says, "He is Jim, she is Fran, and I am Alan." This continues around the class until it comes back to the very first person who then gets to repeat everyone's name.

2. Done the same way but with adding a positive adjective that describes you. "I am funny Jim." "He is funny Jim and I am friendly Fran." This continues till everyone has gone. Again the first person gets to repeat them.

OPTION

Can be done with adding on something you are good at doing, (i.e., "I am softball playing Tom.")

CLUMP

Students are asked to move freely about an open area in the room. The group leader calls out a number such as "Clump Eight." Everyone must clump together in groups of eight. "Clump Four" would suggest that they group together in fours.

Physical contact must be made (i.e., joining hands, arms around shoulders, etc.) After five seconds, the leader calls "freeze", and looks about to find those not in a clump. Anyone not in a clump of the designated number is "out." The game continues until only three or four players remain.

OPTION

1. Have a student be the "caller" for the second or third game of Clump.

2. Introduce "Clump One" before starting. "Clump One" is hugging yourself!

3. Have students who are "out" assist in counting clump groups when "freeze" is called.

BIRTHDAY PARTY

Directions to the class: "Imagine this is your birthday and each of you have called everyone together for a giant birthday party. You know everybody here, but nobody else knows anybody at all. Since it's your party and you want to have fun, you want us all to meet each other. Your task in the next few minutes is to introduce everybody here to everybody else. You are not to introduce yourself to anybody.

For example, you can go up to someone and say,
"Hi, what's your name?"
("Robert.")
"Hi Robert, come with me, I'd like you to meet somebody."

Now go up to another person and say,
"Hi, what's your name?"
("Denise.")
"Hiya Denise, this is Robert. Robert this is Denise."

Now, when you get introduced to somebody, really do it with a lot of energy. Look at the person; shake hands, give a big smile. You have just a few minutes to introduce everybody here to one another! Everyone is introducing people all at the same time. It is your birthday party, so go for it!

(Enthusiasm is the key in introducing the game. It's usually lots of fun!)

KNOTS

Knots is a fun game which allows for non-threatening touching and group cooperation.

The game works best in groups of 8 or 9, the minimum being 7, and the maximum being 13. To start, each group stands in a circle, shoulder-to-shoulder, and places all hands in the center. Now everybody grabs a couple of hands. Make sure no one holds both hands of the same person or holds the hand of a person right next to them. It might take a bit of switching around to get the knot tied right. That's part of the fun.

The object is to unravel so that the circle is reformed with all people holding hands, without any knots. Pivoting on the hands without letting go is allowed. The circles may wind up facing in or out or a combination. Sometimes even two unknotted circles may be the result. Usually everyone figures it out within 3-5 minutes. As a last ditch resort, legitimate cheating can be suggested. "On the count of 3 everyone in your group can drop hands and quickly join hands with the person next to them."

HAND SQUEEZE

This activity can be done for groups of up to about 150 people. Everyone is in a circle holding hands. The leader gently squeezes the hand of the person next to him/her (on one side). As soon as that person feels his/her hand squeezed, he/she squeezes the hand of the next person; and so on as the squeeze is quickly passed around. This happens non-verbally, quickly and gently around the circle. One variation is that once the squeeze is moving in one direction, the leader can send a squeeze moving in the other direction.

OTHER VARIATIONS

1. Passing the sound "ooh" in one direction and "aah" in the other
2. Passing a funny face with a noise
3. Passing an imaginary object
4. Timing how fast the squeeze moves

TIGER, EAGLE, LOVING PERSON

Break into trios. This is a game where silliness is the rule. ("Is everyone willing to act silly?"). Demonstrate the three positions. Turn your back to group and jump around, facing them, as you demonstrate each:

Tiger - ("Growl" and hands poised like a tiger attacking.)

Pistol - ("Pow" and hands like two toy guns shooting.)

Loving person - (Turn around and blow kisses or arm gesture reaching out to others.)

Have the group practice each with you as you do it. Have the class divide into groups of three. Have each group form triangles, shoulder to shoulder, facing out. Without any words their task is to nonverbally send a message to all in their trio so that they all choose the same choice. Now everyone counts down "3-2-1" and jumps around, shouts and acts out their choice. The object is for all in the group to match up. More than that, it's a way for people to have fun and get to know each other.

SHARING CIRCLE

Get into a big circle with everyone's arms around each other's waists or shoulders. The group starts taking small steps to the left, and keeps going to the left until somebody says "Stop!" Then that person shares their name and a positive statement. They might want to say something positive about how they feel or about what they have learned. They might want to express appreciation for another person or for the whole group.

When they've finished their brief sharing, they say "Go." Everyone take small steps in the other direction until someone else says "Stop!" and shares something she or he is feeling good about. When you have a sense that everyone who wants to take a turn has taken a turn (and not everyone has to go, of course) then you say "Stop!" and you ask "Are we done yet?" If someone in the circle still has something more to share with the group, then that person says, "No, Go!" Everyone continues moving around in the circle, and someone else can ask the question again later. If the question is followed by ten seconds of silence, you know that the game is over. Everyone can then give themselves a standing ovation.

GIVING & RECEIVING

This game works best in groups of three. It can be done with people of all ages and takes about 15 to 20 minutes. It's a great process for asking for what you want, giving to others, and allowing others to give to you.

The groups of threes can be sitting either on the floor or in chairs.

Have the groups decide who is going to be Partner A, Partner B, and Partner C (or Chocolate Cake, Strawberry Cheesecake, and Hot Fudge Sundae).

Partner A will be first. Partner A's task is to give Partners B and C instructions and tasks to do that will create a room full of support, caring, appreciation, and fun. This person will first tell their two partners what they would like them to give away (e.g., "Partner B, I'd like you to go give three people a hug and then come back for further directions." "Partner C, I'd like you to go tell four people they look great today and then come back for further directions."). Other examples are telling jokes, singing songs, massaging shoulders, etc. Partners B and C start giving.

After three minutes, call time. Then for the next two minutes, Partner A gets to ask Partners B and C for anything that he/she wants for him/herself (i.e., a shoulder massage, hug, compliments, etc.). Partners B and C give to Partner A.

Then repeat the process with Partners B and then C taking the lead.

(This game creates a lot of lighthearted fun and caring in the room. Generally a favorite. Other categories besides desserts can be used, i.e., types of flowers, music, ice cream flavors, etc.)

CLASS CONTRACT

PURPOSE

1. To develop group cohesiveness.

2. To establish norms for classroom interaction.

3. To enhance cooperation.

4. To develop personal responsibility for rules.

PROCEDURE

1. Lead the students in a discussion of what kind of qualities and characteristics they would like to see in their class this year.

2. Discuss the need for guidelines to help create this kind of atmosphere. Ask students to think about what ground rules would facilitate the kind of interaction they would like in the class.

3. Have students generate these one at a time. When a ground rule is proposed, such as "Listening attentively when someone is speaking" or "Not talking when someone has the floor," ask if they will agree to the rule. If they have objections, encourage them to voice them now for discussion because they will be asked to commit to the ground rules.

4. When an objection is raised, see if the rule can be rewritten in such a way as to allow full commitment of the student objecting and still be consistent with the qualities of interaction established by the class. Ask the class for assistance in finding a way to do this. If this is not possible, assist the student in seeing how they can be "true" to themselves and still work within the needs of the class rule.

5. Continue until a satisfactory list of ground rules has been developed by the class, soliciting commitment to abide by them along the way and entertaining objections as they arise. Suggest any additions you feel are important and solicit agreement.

6. When the list of ground rules is complete have the list typed. Have every class member sign on that one list as a contract to abide by.

7. Duplicate the signed copy and distribute the list to each student. Post a copy in the classroom.

DISCUSSION

1. Are you typically someone who likes rules? dislikes rules?

2. Do you usually keep or break rules?

3. Do you usually feel as if rules are made for you or against you?

4. How did you feel during this activity? Did you get involved in "forming" your rules?

5. How was the way all of you developed the class rules done differently than usual? Was your attitude different than usual?

6. What did you learn about the class? about yourself?

OPTION

1. When a new student comes into your classroom (mid-semester) review ground rules with them. Ask him/her to sign the original contract (list) and then make a new copy for each student in the class.

2. Incorporate rewards for following the ground rules and consequences for breaking them.

LANDMARKS IN MY LIFE

PURPOSE

1. To explore the major events in students' lives that contribute to their behavior and attitudes.

2. To build group cohesiveness.

PROCEDURE

1. See activity sheet for directions.

2. Ask for volunteers and choose who will go first, second, etc.

3. Determine how much time each board will be up. Be sure each student will have a board up.

4. Provide bulletin board space.

5. Give students 1 week or more to prepare.

6. Have students write an explanation of how each event contributes to their present attitudes and behavior. This may be part of the board or done later.

7. You may want to do a board too!

DISCUSSION

Students are encouraged to acknowledge themselves for their work and self-exploration. Discussion around put-downs is in order if students begin to do comparative or negative judgments on their boards or those of others.

- When comparing we always come out on the short end.
- This is an exploring process not one of artistic perfection.
- What's going on inside of you when you're comparing or when judgments come up?

LANDMARKS IN MY LIFE

Design a bulletin board about the major landmarks, events or changes in your life that you feel have contributed to how you now think and behave. If you are aware of future changes you'd like to make, add a section to show these, too.

Example: If your family moved when you were five, and you learned how to make new friends, you might include pictures of yourself at five, drawings of you and your friends, a floor plan of your new house, or a poem about your first outing with a new friend.

Some possible items to include are listed below:

- Pictures - baby pictures, class pictures, family pictures, pictures of you with your pets, pictures of places where you have lived or visited, pictures of you enjoying your hobbies, or pictures of you with your friends

- Awards or ribbons from contests, competitions or events in which you have participated

- Creative work of which you are proud - compositions, poems, artwork, etc.

- Postcards of places you have visited

- Magazine pictures of what you'd like to do or become, of things that are important to you, or of situations or events that have affected your life

GETTING TO KNOW SOMEONE

PURPOSE

1. To strengthen communication skills.

2. To build acceptance of others.

3. To provide a structure for students to move beyond prejudices and find the value in others.

PROCEDURE

1. Each student interviews a classmate, preferably one they do not know well.

2. Students may use the interview questions provided or some of their own. Teachers may want to highlight specific questions for everyone to use.

3. Students devise a method of sharing the information they've gathered with others from a point of view that "This Person is Worth Getting to Know."

Some suggestions: Newspaper article, a positive gossip column, a collage, a mural, a song, a poem, a simulated "Up Close and Personal" TV spot, or an oral report to the class.

4. Students may do their project alone or with their partner. Encourage creativity and fun.

DISCUSSION

1. How did it feel at first to be partners with someone you didn't know well before?

2). What prejudices did you have to overcome?

3. Explore the "walls" we put between ourselves and others for reasons of safety, comfort, etc.

4. Explore how your feelings changed about yourself and the interviewee by getting to know them.

5. How much of a risk was it?

6. Examine how this experience can be taken out of the classroom context. What are the fears, concerns, etc. that come up? How can they be handled?

7. How did the attitude of "this person is worth getting to know" affect your feelings or your project outcome?

8. Have students meet with their partners to express appreciation and learning from the activity.

GETTING TO KNOW SOMEONE

SAMPLE INTERVIEW QUESTIONS

1. What was your childhood nickname and how did you feel about it?
2. Do you like your first name now? If not, what would you like instead?
3. What is the funniest thing that ever happened to you?
4. What is the silliest thing you have ever done?
5. How would you describe yourself?
6. What things have you done that you're proud of?
7. What is the stupidest thing you have ever done?
8. What is your all-time favorite movie? Why does it have special meaning for you?
9. How would your parents have described you as a child (6 to 12)?
10. What was your favorite toy as a child?
11. Who is your best friend of the same sex?
12. Who is your best friend of the other sex?
13. What do you look for most in a friend?
14. What is your favorite possession?
15. Can you name a favorite possession you no longer possess, and describe your feelings about no longer having it?
16. Are you a good friend? Give an example.
17. With what member of your family do you most identify? Why?
18. What is your favorite book? What in it has personal meaning for you?
19. If you had to be someone else instead of yourself, whom would you choose? Why?
20. What in life is most important to you?
21. What do you like most about this class?
22. What do you like least about this class?
23. How would you change this class to make it better?
24. Name something you hate to do. What do you hate about it?
25. Name three reasons why you are worth getting to know.

MEET SOMEONE UNIQUE

PURPOSE

1. To get to know new people.

2. To build group cohesion and acceptance.

3. To build self-esteem and appreciation for each person's uniqueness.

PROCEDURE

1. This is an alternative activity to "Getting to Know Someone." Ask people to stand up and look for someone they do not know well. Tell them to invite such a person to be their partner.

2. Have each person interview the other one for three-five minutes, listening attentively so they will remember important unique qualities and details about the person.

3. After time is up, regroup as a whole and ask each person to introduce the person he/she interviewed by sharing special things learned.

DISCUSSION

1. How did you feel being interviewed by your partner?

2. What was it like to be an interviewer?

3. Did you choose your partner or were you chosen?

4. How do you feel now in contrast to when you first arrived?

5. What have you learned about yourself?

MAP AUTOBIOGRAPHY

PURPOSE

1. To create a visual review of one's life.

2. To build empathy and encourage listening.

PROCEDURE

1. With colored pencils or markers and large sheets of paper, each person draws an illustration, a "map", of the major events, situations, patterns of his/her life to date. Included could be location names, road signs, "high" points, "low" points, places where the road gets twisted and lost and others where the road is straight and defined.

2. Once completed, have the students meet in groups of 5 to 8. Each person shares with the group their map autobiography. The group members offer their support by listening attentively and, after the presenter is through, the group can give feedback and express their feelings and comments.

DISCUSSION

1. Are there any similarities among others' experiences? Differences?

2. Did this help you to know other people in your group better?

3. Did you learn anything about the group as a whole?

4. How did you feel as you made your map? As you shared with the group?

5. Did the group listen while you spoke? How did you know?

6. Did you listen while the others shared?

7. Recall times when people really listened to you or did not listen to you. How did you feel at those times?

LEARNING CHAIN

PURPOSE

1. To enhance listening skills.

2. To provide an opportunity for group members to learn about each other.

3. To encourage cooperative learning in a subject area.

PROCEDURE

1. Divide the class into groups of 5-7 students.

2. One student begins the process by asking another student a question which will help the group know that person better. The person answers and then asks a third person a question about him/herself, and so on, making sure everyone in the group has an opportunity to participate.

3. Remind students to listen fully and caringly to the person sharing. Remind them that they can pass on answering a question if they so choose.

DISCUSSION

1. Did you feel listened to by the group?

2. What did you learn as a listener? As a respondent?

3. What did you enjoy most about this process?

OPTIONS

Have the questions focus on some subject matter that you want students to review. This can be a good activity to prepare for a test.

PHOTO SEARCH

PURPOSE

1. To build a sense of group cohesiveness and fun.

2. To reinforce the concept of change and growth.

PROCEDURE

1. Ask the students to bring in a baby/childhood photo that they are willing to have displayed for a few months. Have them print their names neatly on the back of the photos. The photos can be mounted on colored construction paper and posted on a bulletin board. Each photo can be numbered and an answer key posted on the bulletin board as well.

2. If a student does not have a childhood photo, you may take and print a cell phone photo of them in a disguise so that they may be included.

OPTION

Create a "Guess Who" photo bulletin board with everyone in a disguise or dressed in the clothes that depict their "ideal future career or profession." These photos can be done at home or make a photo day of it in class.

FREE ADVICE

PURPOSE

1. To privately let go of a troubling concern.

2. To accept others' points of view.

3. To value your own point of view.

PROCEDURE

1. Pass out an index card to everyone upon which students neatly write a problem or a concern that they are having about a real situation in their life. It might deal with friends, family, school, etc. They are not to write their names on it.

2. The cards are all collected and then the problems are read aloud one at a time.

3. Ask the students to share their ideas on how they'd best advise that unknown person in solving each problem.

DISCUSSION

1. Were you surprised at some of the problems? Solutions?

2. Did you learn any new solutions that you had not thought of before?

3. Were many of the problems ones with which you could identify?

OPTIONS

1. Once the cards are collected, students each pick up one card and read the problem out loud as if it was theirs. Others offer advice.

2. A given area can be focused on: concerns dealing with boyfriends/girlfriends, grades, brothers/sisters, parents, sex, drugs, etc.

3. Rather than having solutions shared aloud, each student can write their private advice column (a la "Dear Abby") in response.

4. Form small groups. Brainstorm solutions to the problem. A group spokesperson shares with the whole group.

5. Integrate into subject matter, by giving advice to historical or literary characters.

MYSTERY PERSON

PURPOSE

To increase students' awareness of themselves and each other. This is excellent as a fun "getting to know you" activity.

PROCEDURE

1. On a card have the students neatly print some (5 to 10) biographical clues that describe themselves without making it too obvious who they are. Clues can include special talents, favorite hobbies or interests, particular goals or dreams, unusual information about their personal or family history, likes or dislikes, favorite music, musicians or bands, movie stars, positive personal qualities, etc. It is fun to have the teacher include a card for him/herself as well.

2. The cards are collected and each day, or week, a card is read while the class makes guesses at who the "mystery" person is. You can have a student read the "mystery" person card.

DISCUSSION

1. What is something new that you have learned about the "mystery" person?

2. Which clue gave it away?

3. What clue would have revealed the "mystery" person had it been given?

4. What similarities between the "mystery" person and yourself did you discover?

IF YOU ONLY KNEW

PURPOSE

1. To allow self-disclosure and sharing with low risk.

2. To build cohesion in the group.

PROCEDURE

1. On the board write a series of questions such as:

    - What I am most afraid of is . . . .
    - The thing I find hardest to admit is . . .
    - My most embarrassing moment was . . . .
    - What I am secretly proud of is . . . .

2. Distribute index cards to each student and ask them to complete one of the statements listed. Tell them to print their sentences because the answers will be shared anonymously. Encourage them to share something they normally would not. Ask them not to write their names on the cards.

3. Collect the cards and redistribute them to the group.

4. Read all answers written to complete the first sentence, then go on to the second, etc.

DISCUSSION

1. Did you hear similarities in the responses?

2. Did you experience things that you did not share which were similar to the responses read? How did it feel to hear it shared by someone else?

3. What did you learn from this?

SECRET BUDDY

PURPOSE

1. To build relationships based on caring and fun.

2. To experience the fun of giving.

PROCEDURE

1. Each person, including the teacher writes his/her name neatly on a small slip of paper and folds it up.

2. Place all the slips in a hat or box.

3. Each person takes a name from the hat (returning it if it is his/her own name). Keep the identity of your secret buddy a secret!

4. Begin by playing the game for a short time - a day, or a week. The group can decide. Later, when you play again, playing for a couple of weeks or a month can be fun.

5. For the time period chosen, do friendly things for your secret buddy.

- Give a surprise gift or card
- Clean up after them
- Help them with some work
- Buy them lunch before they get to the register

Be creative and have fun with the process of giving from your friendliness. Enjoy the giving and the receiving.

6. When the time period is up have buddies identify themselves to each other and spend some time sharing about the experience and expressing their appreciation.

DISCUSSION

Group sharing may occur spontaneously. Watch for comparing (i.e., "your buddy was better than mine"), awkwardness, hurt feelings, and communication methods. If necessary, take the time to discuss these in the large group or individually.

OPTIONS

This is a great activity for the students to do with their families. Review with them ways they can introduce it to their family. Have them share later on about the results.

GRAB BAG

PURPOSE

1. To build group trust.

2. To encourage personal sharing.

PROCEDURE

1. Ask students to divide into groups of 5-8 and to sit in a circle in their group.

2. Pass pre-prepared bags (one for each group) containing question slips to each group. Each slip has a question such as, "When are you really happy?", "What is the most special positive quality about you?", "When have you felt very proud?". Be sure there is one slip for each group member, plus a few extra. Ask people to draw the questions with eyes closed.

3. People have the "right to return" if they do not like the question that they have drawn and may select another one from those that remain in the bag after the bag has made it around the group. They put the original slip back after taking a new one.

4. Have students take turns reading and answering their questions. Remind people of their right to pass if they do not want to answer the question.

DISCUSSION

1. Does anyone want more information from someone who shared? (if so, then ask; again the person has the right to pass.)

2. Would anyone like to respond to a question that someone else drew?

3. Was it hard to share?

4. Did others listen? How did you know? Did you listen?

5. Did it get easier as you went along?

OPTIONS

This game can be used to review subject matter by writing appropriate questions on the slips.

HOT SEAT

PURPOSE

1. To build group cohesiveness.

2. To practice communication skills.

3. To share personal beliefs, feelings and interests.

PROCEDURE

1. Ask all to sit in a circle.

2. One person will sit in the middle of the circle (the hot seat) and answer three questions from the group. The person can pass if they do not want to answer a question. He/she will choose the questions from people who raise their hands.

3. You be the first one in the circle to model the activity.

4. Questions may be autobiographical or may relate to issues, curriculum, politics, hobbies, friendships, sports.

5. Have as many students take turns in the Hot Seat as seems appropriate.

DISCUSSION

1. Can we generalize about the types of questions asked?

2. Did this activity help you to know group members better?

3. How did you feel being interviewed?

4. Did the group listen? How did you know?

5. Do you have any appreciations for anyone after this exercise? Go ahead and share it.

SPEAKING OUT

PURPOSE

To provide an opportunity to encourage students and teacher to express their views on subjects of their choice.

PROCEDURE

1. Discuss the concept of "Speaking Out."

    a) This is an opportunity to regularly share ideas and opinions with others without being interrupted.

    b) Clarify your thinking on an issue. Everyone has a right to their own ideas and ways of seeing things.

    c) If you are really concerned about something, speak up and express your views. Take advantage of the opportunity to increase others' awareness.

    d) This is an opportunity to listen and be open to different subjects, viewpoints and to reconsider how you see an issue.

    e) This will give you an opportunity to see what issues, concerns and problems are important to the class.

2. Guidelines for "Speaking Out".

    a) When speaking out on a problem, present at least one solution.

    b) Have main point(s) prepared before speaking out.

    c) Time allotted is 1-3 minutes per "speaking out."

    d) When "speaking out," practice using "I - statements" to own your views and feelings. There is no need to use put downs or to attack.

    e) When listening to the person speaking out, be open to learning from other points of view. If you have a different perspective prepare a rebuttal.

3. Set up a "soapbox": i.e., a wooden box, a high stool, or a certain chair to stand on will do.

4. Designate a regular time each week/month for "speaking out."

5. Possible topics for speaking out:

    • Classroom or campus issues

    • Community issues

    • National and world issues (i.e., homeless, environment, etc.)

    • Specific current events

    • Personal issues

OPTION

Integrate with subject material, historical events, politics, or famous literary and historical characters.

CASTLES IN THE CLASS

PURPOSE

1. To develop an awareness of one's behavior in a group.

2. To explore non-verbal communication.

3. To build group cohesiveness.

PROCEDURE

1. Divide the class into groups of 5 students.

2. Pass out 15-20 pieces of 8-1/2" x 11" paper and 1 roll of tape to each group. Tell the students that they are to non-verbally construct a tower or castle using only the given supplies, and that they will have 10 minutes to complete the task.

3. At the end of 10 minutes, stop the action.

4. Have all the groups view each other's buildings.

5. Ask them to return to their groups for discussion (which is an important part of this activity).

6. Have all group members thank one another and acknowledge themselves for their work.

DISCUSSION

First, pose questions #1-4 for the individual groups to discuss. Then open up for large group discussion of questions #5 and #6.

1. Did your group have enough materials? Would more or less be helpful?

2. What was happening in your group? Who started the building? Did leaders change? Did any people just give up?

3. What non-verbal signals were people giving to each other either concerning the tower or their feelings?

4. How do you feel about what happened? Pleased? Frustrated?

5. What did you learn about yourself? Is this your usual style in working with others? Are you an effective team member? How could you improve?

6. What does it take for team projects to work well?

GREAT PERSON OF THE YEAR

PURPOSE

1. To foster positive feelings among class members.

2. To build self-esteem.

PROCEDURE

1. Everyone in the class writes his/her name on a piece of paper and drops it into a basket. Each person draws a name out of the basket. He/She is the "promoter" for the person whose name he/she has drawn. The person has been nominated for the "Great Person of the Year" award.

2. Each promoter meets with his/her candidate and gathers information about what makes them so very great (i.e., their special qualities, traits, and/or abilities).

3. Each "promoter" delivers his/her nomination speech and presents his/her nominee to the entire group. The class offers applause, cheering and encouragement. EVERYONE IS A WINNER.

DISCUSSION

1. What did you learn in your interviews?

2. Did you notice any similarities between the campaign speech that you gave and the one given about you?

3. How did you feel when you promoted your candidate?

4. How did you feel being presented? Shy? Embarrassed? Proud?

CHAPTER 2
Building Self-Esteem

TEACHING TIPS & SUGGESTIONS

1 The easiest and most lasting way for students to change their behavior is by changing their self-image. Rather than a self-image of, "It is like me to fail or to get in trouble," the self-concept becomes, "It is like me to get excellent grades and to get along with others . . . It is natural for me to do well."

2 Recognize that "bad" behavior and acting out are symptomatic of low self-esteem. Shyness, isolation, discouragement, disinterest, anger, challenges to authority, bullying, hypersensitivity and blaming are just some of the many behaviors that result from low self-esteem. As you deal appropriately with the symptomatic behavior, realize that the steady work of building that student's self-image will be the most lasting remedy.

3 Foster group support during activities by asking the class to frequently practice acknowledging each other. For example, "Everyone, let's give Connie a hand for her leadership on that project."

4 Make it okay for students to "pass" when it is their assigned turn to share in an activity. Sometimes, gentle and playful encouragement from you or the class can support them into taking a risk and speaking. However, give them the freedom to choose back.

5 Differentiate between self-acknowledgment and being conceited. Students typically are wary of being seen as conceited, and often confuse positive self-image with conceit. Discuss the difference. Self-acknowledgment is not built upon the reference of being better than another or putting someone down to build yourself up (i.e., "I am an excellent teacher," vs. "I am the best teacher in the school, and no one else comes close."). This discussion will often bring up students' fear of disapproval from their peers. Also, it can lead into an excellent discussion of how they might sometimes base their self-worth on opinions from others rather than on their own self-approval and self-valuing. Know that self-acknowledgment exercises may at first seem unusual for the student, yet they are extremely valuable.

6 Watch for negative self-talk and put-downs. Have everyone scouting for these "killer statements," and when they are spotted, experiment with having them switched to affirming statements. (i.e., "Nothing is going right for me today," changes to "I am doing my best at handling my challenges today.").

7 Find a variety of ways to incorporate affirmations and creative visualizations into the daily routine. (One seventh grade math class started their class out each morning with a different student leading the class in a short "rap song" version of their class affirmation: "Math is fun and easy." What a great alternative to the more commonly heard self-talk: "Math is boring and hard.")

8 Create numerous opportunities for special awards, acknowledgments, and celebrations. Find ways so that, over time, everyone is included.

ACTIVITY PREVIEWS

APPRECIATION
Focus: Written activity to acknowledge appreciation to yourself and significant others.
Time: 10-15 minutes
Activity: Page II-05

BE A FRIEND TO YOURSELF
Focus: Written activity to treat yourself as you would a best friend.
Time: 15-20 minutes
Activity: Page II-07

POSITIVE QUALITIES
Focus: List positive qualities about yourself.
Time: 10-15 minutes
Activity: Page II-09

GOOD NEWS
Focus: Self-acknowledgment to be reinforced by sharing with yourself and others.
Time: 15 minutes
Activity: Page II-11

BRAGGING
Focus: Take time to brag to yourself about how terrific you are.
Time: 5-10 minutes
Activity: Page II-13

UNSTRUCTURED WRITING
Focus: Express and let go of negative feelings and problems through unstructured, spontaneous writing.
Time: 10 minutes

ADMIRATION MIRROR
Focus: Recognize you have the qualities you admire in others.
Time: 15 minutes
Activity: Page II-17

SELF-TALK
Focus: Examine your use of positive and negative self-talk.
Time: 20-30 minutes
Activity: Page II-20

PUTDOWNS
Focus: Through social observation, students explore frequency and effect of putdowns in their lives.
Time: 20-30 minutes in class time, additional out of class time.

LETTING GO
Focus: Letting go of self-judgments.
Time: 30 minutes
Activity: Page II-26

KEEPING TRACK OF NEGATIVE SELF-TALK
Focus: Monitor negative self-talk while developing observation skills.
Time: 30 minutes

PRACTICING POSITIVE SELF-TALK
Focus: Explore the power of self-talk and practice positive self-talk.
Time: 20-30 minutes in class, additional out of class time.
Activity: Page II-30

SELF-FORGIVENESS
Focus: Taking time to forgive yourself to allow for more self acceptance.
Time: 20 minutes
Activity: Page II-33

POSITIVE FEEDBACK CARDS
Focus: Give and receive positive feedback and appreciation in a supportive atmosphere.
Time: 20-25 minutes

ACKNOWLEDGMENT
Focus: Ask for and receive acknowledgment from yourself and a partner.
Time: 15-20 minutes

AFFIRMATIONS
Focus: Explore the concept and use of positive affirmations.
Time: 30-40 minutes
Activity: Page II-38

STUDENT AFFIRMATION
Focus: Develop positive self-concept through repetition of a positive affirmation.
Time: 5 minutes (suggested daily)
Activity: Page II-41

ADVERTISING ME
Focus: Acknowledge and share each person's uniqueness.
Time: 1 week
Activity: Page II-43

COME ON DOWN
Focus: Build self-esteem through mock T.V. game show.
Time: 30 minutes

I AM GRATEFUL FOR
Focus: List the things in life for which you are thankful.
Time: 10 minutes
Activity: Page II-47

GRATITUDE
Focus: Become aware of all there is to be grateful for in life.
Time: 15 minutes
Activity: Page II-49

SUPER ME CAPE
Focus: Give statements of appreciation and support in an interactive written activity.
Time: 30-40 minutes

LETTER TO YOURSELF
Focus: Write a letter of caring support and encouragement to brighten a day in the future.
Time: 15 minutes
Activity: Page II-53

SUPER BOOSTER
Focus: Give and receive positive feedback in an interactive verbal class activity.
Time: 30-40 minutes

MAKING THE BEST OF ME | CHAPTER 2: II-03

APPRECIATION

PURPOSE

1. To become aware of what you appreciate about yourself and others.

2. To practice taking time to express these appreciations.

3. To enhance self-esteem.

PROCEDURE

Students complete activity sheet.

APPRECIATION

Taking time to appreciate yourself and others is a powerful tool to enhance your self-esteem.

For example, what I appreciate about myself is:

    1. My being a good friend
    2. My courage
    3. My self-discipline
    4. My honesty
    5. My sense of humor

What I appreciate about **myself** is:

1.
2.
3.
4.
5.

What I appreciate about _____ is:
(friend's name)

1.
2.
3.
4.
5.

What I appreciate about _____ is:
(family member's name)

1.
2.
3.
4.
5.

What I appreciate about _____ is:
(family member's name)

1.
2.
3.
4.
5.

MAKING THE BEST OF ME | **CHAPTER 2: II-05**

BE A FRIEND TO YOURSELF

PURPOSE

1. To give yourself what you want.

2. To learn to treat yourself as your own best friend.

3. To enhance self-esteem.

PROCEDURE

Students follow directions on activity sheet.

DISCUSSION

1. Are you used to treating yourself this nicely?

2. What would be different in your life if you did?

BE A FRIEND TO YOURSELF

Imagine you have one day to enhance a friend's self-esteem. How would you treat them? What kinds of things would you do and/or say to them? Write a list below:

1.

2.

3.

4.

5.

6.

7.

8.

9.

10.

Now go back and read over your list. How many of the things that you would do for a friend, have you done for yourself in the last two weeks? Circle them on your list. Is it more than half? Less than half? Acknowledge yourself for the things that you have done to be your own good friend.

Someone once said that if we treated our friends the way we treat ourselves, we wouldn't have any friends. If you do more of these things on your list for yourself, you will enhance your own self-esteem.

Now choose something on your list that you want, can, and will do for yourself this week and put a star next to it. Choose a specific time to do this and mark it on your calendar. Remember to check it off once you have completed it.

POSITIVE QUALITIES

PURPOSE

To enhance self-esteem through acknowledging positive qualities.

PROCEDURE

Have students complete activity sheet.

DISCUSSION

Discuss the feelings students have about acknowledging themselves. Is it easy? hard? Suggest practice.

POSITIVE QUALITIES

Make a list of at least 20 positive qualities about yourself.

For example, I am:

    1. kind
    2. happy
    3. intelligent
    4. honest

I am:

1.

2.

3.

4.

5.

6.

7.

8.

9.

10.

11.

12.

13.

14.

15.

16.

17.

18.

19.

20.

GOOD NEWS

PURPOSE

1. To list and share the good news about yourself.

2. To increase awareness of positive qualities.

PROCEDURE

1. Students complete activity sheet.

2. Students share the good news about themselves with:

    a) A friend or partner.

    b) Privately with yourself in front of a mirror.

    c) A family member.

DISCUSSION

1. How did you feel about writing or speaking positively about yourself?

2. Do you usually spend your time in negative or positive self-talk?

3. What do people get from speaking negatively about themselves? (People wouldn't do it unless there was a payoff; i.e., other people feeling sorry for them, etc.)

4. What do you have to risk when you think or speak positively of yourself? Is it worth it?

OPTIONS

Do the Good News activity as a small or large group sharing process. Have people stand up, one at a time, and share, "The Good News about me is . . . ." Each person gets a big applause as they sit down.

NOTE

This activity can often slip into "What I like . . . ." Make sure to keep everyone on track in their sharing what is good about them or what they are good at doing.

GOOD NEWS

Make a list of at least 20 positive qualities about yourself.

For example, The good news about me is:

    1. I am a good student.
    2. I am a very enthusiastic person.
    3. I am a caring and trustworthy friend.
    4. I am handsome/pretty.
    5. I am funny, and people have fun when they are with me.

The good news about me is:

1.

2.

3.

4.

5.

6.

7.

8.

9.

10.

11.

12.

13.

14.

15.

16.

17.

18.

19.

20.

MAKING THE BEST OF ME | **CHAPTER 2: II-11**

BRAGGING

PURPOSE
To build a habit of acknowledging oneself for large and small accomplishments.

PROCEDURE
Students follow directions on activity sheet.

BRAGGING

This process can be done by speaking out loud in front of a mirror, by writing a list, or by sitting back silently with your eyes closed - whichever way you prefer. Take three minutes each day to brag about yourself to yourself. Review all the great things you did today and how wonderful you are. These can be little things like helping someone at home, complimenting someone at school, or picking up trash in your neighborhood. You can brag about some of the good things you have done for yourself like eating healthy foods and taking care of yourself, or you can brag about some of the things you are grateful for like getting the grades you wanted, having wonderful friendships, getting along better with your family, and so forth.

The great things I did today are:

1.

2.

3.

4.

5.

6.

7.

8.

9.

10.

UNSTRUCTURED WRITING

PURPOSE
To express and let go of negative situations and feelings through writing privately.

PROCEDURE
1. Have the students take out a clean piece of paper and ask them to write for 10 minutes about whatever they are thinking and feeling. Whatever comes to mind, without trying to figure it out or think about it, they are to just write it down. No one's going to see it. In fact, they are told to not reread what they write. They are not to be concerned in this activity about spelling, or grammar or legibility. Instruct the students to write about whatever comes to mind without judging it or trying to analyze it. It is okay for them to write about things that are concerning or troubling them. Encourage them to express honestly.

2. At the end of the time allotted, students are to tear up their paper without rereading what they have written. The pieces are thrown into a trash can. This process is often called "emptying out the garbage."

> *Note: Unstructured writing is not to be confused with work done in the students' journals, which is not to be torn up.*

DISCUSSION
How did you feel while writing? How do you feel now? Any changes?

Note: It may not always be best to go back over and have the students analyze the exercise. This process can be a "letting go" experience and refocusing may not be totally beneficial. However, be sensitive to the particular needs of an individual student or the class as a whole.

OPTIONS
1. Do this activity regularly; each day, once a week, etc.

2. This activity can be especially helpful if the class has experienced an emotionally difficult event.

ADMIRATION MIRROR

PURPOSE

1. To recognize the qualities admired in others are also in yourself.

2. To enhance self-esteem.

PROCEDURE

Students complete activity sheet.

DISCUSSION

1. How did it feel owning the positive qualities for yourself?

2. How does the saying "Beauty is in the eyes of the beholder" pertain to this activity?

3. How does this "mirror" concept work regarding seeing the worst in other people?

4. What did you learn about yourself?

OPTIONS

This activity can be done verbally with a partner or in small groups of 5 - 8 people.

ADMIRATION MIRROR

Choose someone you admire. Make a list of the things you admire about them.

I admire _____. The things I admire about him/her are:
    (fill in name)

1.

2.

3.

4.

5.

_____ is a mirror of me. The things I admire about him/her are also true of me.
(fill in the same name)

Therefore: *(copy the same qualities you just wrote, starting each sentence with "I am")*

1.

2.

3.

4.

5.

The ways that I show those qualities in my life are:

MAKING THE BEST OF ME | **CHAPTER 2: II-17**

SELF-TALK

PURPOSE

1. To teach the importance and effects of self-talk.

2. To develop awareness of student's negative and positive self-talk.

PROCEDURE

1. Teach the concept and effects of positive/negative self-talk.

    Sample Introduction:

    Of all the people you talk to in your life, the person you talk to the most is yourself. Each day you have thousands of thoughts and ideas about who you are and what you are doing. The way you think and talk about yourself strongly influences your life.

    As each of us grows up, each day we hear hundreds of negative comments. Research has shown that an average two year old will have ten times more negative comments ("shut up." "no," "that's bad/ wrong.") directed his/her way than positive comments ("thanks," "good going," "great job.") People usually do not intentionally give negative comments. Parents, brothers, sisters, teachers, and friends often have received negative comments throughout their lives and without much awareness of how harmful it is pass it on to others.

    After years of growing up hearing negative comments, people start to believe that they are a lot of what people say they are. We take it to heart and start to believe that maybe we are too tall, too short, too shy, too talkative, too rude, too loud, too disrespectful, too . . . . Inside of our conversation with ourselves ("self-talk"), we create a complicated assortment of ways to doubt and judge ourselves, and get unduly worried about the past or fearful about the future.

    What if you are not responsible for every thought you now have, but only the ones you hold in mind and keep thinking and thinking about?

    Of all the many habits people can choose to have, the negative self-talk habit may be one of the most harmful. For many people it's an addiction. Building the positive self-talk habit takes practice. The more that you develop positive self-talk, positive thinking, positive feeling, and positive actions the more you will enjoy your life.

    With positive self-talk, you are taking great care of yourself. You are making your life be the best you dream it can be.

2. Students complete activity sheet.

    Tell Students:

    In answering the following questions, be honest and give yourself the chance to build the positive self-talk habit.

DISCUSSION

1. Discuss times when class members gave themselves a lot of negative self-talk. Discuss times when they gave themselves a lot of positive self-talk.

2. Why is it easier at times to be negative about yourself than positive?

3. What are ways that the students can help each other build a positive self-talk habit?

SELF-TALK

List at least five negative self-talk statements you tell yourself often.

For example:
"No matter what I do, it is never good enough."
"Nothing is going to go right for me today."
"They/he/she doesn't like me. No one cares really cares about me."

1.
2.
3.
4.
5.

What you say to yourself matters a lot. The more good things you say to yourself the better you feel, and the more self-esteem and confidence you gain.

List at least ten positive self-talk statements you can say about who you are and what you do.

For example:
"I am a great friend who people trust and like."
"I am good at making decisions. I like challenges, and I meet them head on."
"I really am very special. I like who I am, and I feel good about myself."

1.
2.
3.
4.
5.
6.
7.
8.
9.
10.

PUTDOWNS

PURPOSE

1. To sensitize the students to the negative effect of giving and receiving putdowns.

2. To develop observation skills.

PROCEDURE

1. Prepare the class with a discussion on putdowns. Give some of your personal examples of giving and receiving putdowns.

   The sample discussion might cover:

   We all have had times when we have felt put down, when others have directed negative comments our way. At times we have commented negatively back, fought out, or pretended to ignore them. No matter how we have reacted, we often have felt hurt inside. In reality, the common childhood cliche, "Sticks and stones can break my bones, but names can never hurt me." just isn't true.

   Have you ever done something you felt really great about and someone knocked it down with a sarcastic or negative comment?

   What was it? How did you feel?

   Have the tables ever been turned when you've done that to someone else? Why? How did you feel about it while you did? Within yourself, how did you defend what you did to believe you were in the "right?" How did you feel when you did? How do you think the other person felt? After you did it, how did you feel about it?

2. Tell the students that for the next day, they will be doing a putdown research project. As they go though their day, they are each to privately write down at least ten putdowns that they hear. It can be ones they hear in their classes, at lunch, at home, or around their neighborhood. Have them have paper and pen handy to write the comments as they hear them. Bring them to class for discussion.

DISCUSSION

1. Ask students to share what they heard.

2. Were you surprised at what you heard?

3. What are some various forms of putdowns? (i.e., jokes, gestures . . .)

4. How did you feel as you listened to and recorded the putdowns?

5. Why do you think people put others down?

6. Are there things that you or others sometimes want to say but are afraid to disclose so you say a putdown instead?

   For example, "That's okay for a girl," instead of saying, "I like you."

7. Have you ever used putdowns because you've been afraid of others' opinions of you and felt you needed to act "cool" or "tough?"

LETTING GO

PURPOSE

1. To become aware of and release limiting beliefs.

2. To replace limiting beliefs with positive belief statements.

PROCEDURE

Students complete activity sheet.

DISCUSSION

Discuss how this activity felt to students. Some teachers stop and have a debriefing session after each section. Emphasize the importance of repeating the new statements.

LETTING GO

1. On a separate piece of paper write the following:

I'm not good enough to _____ because I'm _____.

Continue writing a paragraph or two about the things in yourself you judge or disapprove of and the reasons you give yourself. Now tear it up and throw it away.

Next, write down these statements on a new sheet of paper.

>"I forgive myself for judging myself."

>"I release and let go of anything I have ever held against myself."

>"I am loving myself, and I am worthy."

Beneath that, sign your name.

Read these statements to yourself several times.

2. On a separate piece of paper write the following:

I am too _____.

Continue writing a paragraph or two about the things in yourself you judge or disapprove of and the reasons you give yourself. Now tear it up and throw it away.

Next, write down these statements:

>"I forgive myself for judging myself."

>"I give myself total unconditional acceptance as a loving and worthy individual."

>"I always do the best I can with what I know."

Beneath that, sign your name.

Read these statements to yourself several times.

3) On a separate piece of paper write the following:

I want to _____ but can't because I'm _____.

Continue writing a paragraph or two about what you want that you believe you can't have, do, or be and the reasons you give yourself. Now tear it up and throw it away.

Next, write down these statements:

"I forgive myself for judging myself."

"I release and let go of all blocks I have placed in the way of my having, doing, or being who and what I want."

"I am loving myself, and I am worthy."

"I can be all that I want to be."

Beneath that, sign your name.

Read these statements to yourself several times.

4) On a separate piece of paper write the following:

I'll never _____ because I'm _____.

Continue writing a paragraph or two about what you want that you believe you can't have, do or be and the reasons you give yourself. Now tear it up and throw it away.

Next, write down these statements:

"I forgive myself for judging myself."

"I release and let go of all blocks I have placed in the way of my having, doing, or being who and what I want."

"I am loving myself, and I am worthy."

"I can be all that I want to be."

Beneath that, sign your name.

Read these statements to yourself several times.

KEEPING TRACK OF NEGATIVE SELF-TALK

PURPOSE

1. To notice the frequency of negative self-talk and learn to shift it to the positive.

2. To develop observation and awareness skills.

PROCEDURE

As a follow-up to the Self-Talk activity, ask students to keep a record of every time they have a negative thought during a fifteen minute time period. This takes a lot of attention to keep focused on that task during the course of fifteen minutes. They are to have an index card handy, and every time they have a negative thought, they make a tally mark on the card.

DISCUSSION

(After they have brought in their tally cards)

1. Were you surprised about how often or how infrequently you had negative self-talk?

2. Were you able to keep yourself focused on your task?

3. What are some ways that you might begin to practice positive self-talk? Are you willing to do that?

OPTIONS

1. Keep the tally card going a for an entire day.

2. Ask the students to write out some of the negative self-talk statements that they noticed.

3. Have them keep tallies for a particular area (i.e., negative self-talk about how they look, how they get along with others, how they feel about their work, etc.)

4. Have each student choose one way to practice positive self-talk and do that for one day. Have them report about that experience.

PRACTICING POSITIVE SELF-TALK

PURPOSE

1. To increase awareness of positive and negative talk to oneself and others.

2. To acknowledge the powerful impact positive and negative talk has in reinforcing traits in oneself and family (or class, or peer groups).

3. To experience shifting negative to positive talk for an extended period of time.

PROCEDURE

1. Students complete the activity sheet.

2. Discuss the answers from the sheet as a class. Remind students this is an awareness activity at this point. There is no need to put themselves down or feel ashamed of any negative talk. We all do negative talk at one time or another. The purpose of this activity is to increase awareness of our negative talk and its effects so we can switch it to positive talk when we choose. Words are very powerful. Our behavior is a result of what we say to ourselves and what we have "bought" that others have said to us. So, it is important to know when we are having a positive or negative influence on ourselves and others.

3. 24 hour assignment: For the next 24 hours control your talk to yourself and others. Stay away from putdowns, sarcasm, and hurtful jokes. Instead, catch yourself and others "being good" and comment on it. Appreciate the nice things, large and small, that you do for others and for yourself. If you slip (and you may, after all you are only human) and find yourself talking negatively to yourself or others, simply stop, appreciate yourself for the awareness, and shift the statements into the positive. Apologize, or acknowledge that you were talking negatively. Remind yourself that you are good at talking positively to yourself and others. Then continue on.

4. After the 24 hours is up, discuss what happened and associated feelings, thoughts, and experiences.

PRACTICING POSITIVE SELF-TALK

1. Write a list of the kinds of things you say to yourself most of the time (i.e., "I'm too short," "I hate walking to school," etc.). Look back over a typical day and list your self-talk. Be honest.

*Go back over your list and before each statement that is positive, write (**P**); and before each statement that is negative, write (**N**).*

2. Write a list of the kinds of things you say to others most of the time (i.e., "Thanks, a lot.", "Leave me alone.", etc.). Once again, be honest.

*Go back over your list and before each statement that is positive, write (**P**); and before each statement that is negative, write (**N**).*

3. What positive habits/characteristics do you and your family reinforce because you continue to describe them to one another? (i.e., "We're a friendly family, we do nice things for others.")

4. What negative habits/characteristics do you and your family reinforce because you continue to describe them to one another? (i.e., "No one in this family can sing, we're all tone deaf.")

5. What have you learned about your self-talk and your family's self-talk?

6. What do you choose to do about it?

SELF-FORGIVENESS

PURPOSE

1. To develop a habit of self-forgiveness.
2. To enhance self-acceptance.

PROCEDURE

Students complete activity sheet.

SELF-FORGIVENESS

Take some quiet time to sit back, perhaps with your eyes closed, and review your day or week. If there is anything that you are judging yourself for, you can just say to yourself inwardly, "I forgive myself for _____." and fill in the blank.

Complete the following sentences about what you judged in yourself.

"I forgive myself for:

"I forgive myself for:

"I forgive myself for:

"I forgive myself for:

What if it is true that you did the best you could have in that situation based on who you were then and all that you knew to do. It has been said, "If you knew better, you would have done better."

Can you learn from the situations in which you have judged yourself? Forgiving yourself for your "mistakes" and learning from them is okay. It is amazing how taking a few minutes to write out self-forgiveness can make a big difference in how you feel about yourself.

Write the following sentence five times and read it to yourself as you do.

"I am accepting myself just as I am, and I am learning to do better and better."

1.
2.
3.
4.
5.

POSITIVE FEEDBACK CARDS

PURPOSE

1. To build self-esteem.

2. To reinforce the concept of appreciation among the class.

PROCEDURE

1. This activity is best after class members know one another fairly well.

2. Ask each member to write his/her first name in the upper corner of an index card.

3. Tell the group to place all cards in a center pile, and have each member draw a card, not divulging whose card they have picked. Have each student then write a thoughtful, positive statement about the person whose name is on the card.

4. All cards are returned to the central pile and the process of drawing and writing is repeated four or five times.

5. After the last turn, return all cards and draw one final time. This time, instead of writing, the student reads all of the remarks written on the card to the whole class, delivering the messages as warmly and sincerely as possible.

6. Have the class give each person receiving the feedback a big round of applause.

DISCUSSION

1. When was the last time you received positive, written feedback from others?

2. Do people usually remember to say nice things about others?

3. How do you feel receiving positive statements?

4. How do you feel giving positive statements?

5. How could you apply this with your friends and family?

ACKNOWLEDGMENT

PURPOSE

1. To ask for what you want.

2. To receive the acknowledgment desired.

3. To enhance self-esteem.

PROCEDURE

1. Students neatly write a list of things they would like to be acknowledged for by someone important in their lives.

2. Students exchange lists with another student. Each of them acknowledges the other for what they have written on their list. For example, "James, I acknowledge you for babysitting your little sister. I acknowledge you for getting your English report turned in on time."

3. With the same partner, each student takes their sheet back. Partner A then reads out loud to Partner B his self acknowledgments. "I acknowledge myself for babysitting my little sister. I acknowledge myself for getting my English report turned in on time." Once Partner A has read his/her list of self-acknowledgments out loud, Partner B does the same.

DISCUSSION

1. How did it feel to be acknowledged by another?

2. How did it feel to acknowledge yourself to another?

3. Were you concerned with others thinking you are "conceited?"

4. What's the difference between "conceit" and practicing positive self-acknowledgment?

OPTIONS

1. Students can stand and declare one of their acknowledgments to the whole group (i.e., "I acknowledge myself for . . . ."). Have the class support each sharing with applause.

2. Students can practice reading their self-acknowledgment statements at home while looking in a mirror.

AFFIRMATIONS

PURPOSE

1. To introduce the principle of positive affirmations.

2. To practice creating and using positive affirmations.

PROCEDURE

1. Review the activity sheet with the students.

2. Discuss the concept and use of positive affirmations.

DISCUSSION

1. How can you use affirmations to assist you in sports, schoolwork, and friendships?

2. Discuss the following statement as it pertains to using positive affirmation: "Energy follows thought."

3. How did you feel writing positive affirmations?

OPTIONS

1. Students can write their five favorite affirmations on index cards, take them home, and hide them in their bedroom so that they can find them "by accident" in the weeks to come.

2. Have students decorate the sheet on which they have written their favorite affirmation. Have them hang it in their home so they can see it and read it often.

3. Each day a different student reads his/her affirmation to the class and the class supports the student by repeating it five times out loud. (Example: "Jeff, you are an intelligent, handsome and capable person.")

4. Students write a favorite affirmation of theirs on a card, and everyone mingles around the classroom and finds a partner. Students exchange cards and they read back the other's affirmation. (Example: "James, you are a happy, confident and honest person.") This continues around the room as many times as possible before time is called.

5. Students can write, record, and perform an "Affirmation Song." They can perform it for the class.

6. Students mingle around the classroom and introduce themselves by their affirmation. (Example: "I am Nan, and I am a responsible and hardworking student.") The person that is listening responds enthusiastically, "That's right, you are!" Mingling continues until time is called.

7. They can write an affirmation poem.

8. Students can put their favorite affirmations on audio cassettes, individually or as a class, and listen to them often.

9. They can write an affirmation on a slip of paper and place it in their sock. Throughout the day they'll be reminded of it as they walk.

10. As students exercise, suggest that they repeat their affirmation silently and often. (Rather than, "I am tired and slow," energetically say, "I am healthy, happy, and strong.")

11. Each day for a month, have them write the same affirmation 20 times in a journal. Suggest that they say it silently or out loud each time they write the affirmation.

AFFIRMATIONS

Henry Ford once said, "Whether you think you can or you think you can't, you're probably right!"

It has often been said that "...as a man thinketh in his heart, he becometh."

The words and thoughts that run through our minds are important. Do you let your self-talk dwell on the positive or do you dwell on the negative?

Affirmations are one of the most powerful ways to develop positive self-talk. An affirmation is a story; a statement of positive fact. It is always worded in the present tense and usually begins with "I am..." Affirmations are a way of "making firm" positive things about yourself. By practicing affirmations you can replace negative self-talk with more positive ideas and self-talk.

Positive affirmations develop positive attitudes which create positive feelings which encourage positive actions. You can create a happier and more rewarding life for yourself by practicing positive affirmations. Affirmations can be written, spoken, done silently, recorded on a cassette tape, or sung out loud.

HERE ARE SOME EXAMPLES:

- I have a winning personality. I am friendly, sensitive and real.
- I am loving and supporting myself and receiving love from my family and friends.
- I take great care of myself so I can be the best person I can be.
- I deserve the very best, and I get it.
- I am confident, honest, and trustworthy. I trust myself, and others can count on me.
- I am worthy of having great friends. I am the kind of person people love to be around.
- I am very special. I like who I am. I feel great about myself.
- I am intelligent. My mind is quick and alert. I think good thoughts and I feel happy feelings.
- Today is a great day. I am choosing to live today with confidence.

SOME TIPS ON USING AFFIRMATIONS ARE:

1. Always phrase them in the present tense, not in the future.

For example, rather than saying, "I will be getting higher grades in school," say, "I am getting higher grades in school." Write/think/say it as if it is already happening.

2. Phrase affirmations in a positive way.

For example, rather than saying, "I won't overeat," say, "I am eating wisely and lightly."

3. Keep affirmations specific, powerful, and emotionally dynamic.

4. Affirmations work when you work them. Repeat them often, in different ways. Have fun with your affirmations.

5. Practice your affirmations with a lot of energy and enthusiasm. Use as many of your senses as possible. Read them, write them, say them aloud, and listen to them. Put a lot of feeling into them. Let them come alive!

6. Affirmations work best when they are coupled with action. Take the necessary action to make your affirmations true in your daily life. (A student who affirms that "I am passing this test," is advised to study for the test as well!) Affirmation and action go hand in hand.

Write a list of five positive, inner qualities you would like to develop more of *(Example: patience, courage, acceptance of myself)*:

1.

2.

3.

4.

5.

Write a personal affirmation for each quality *(Example: "I am patient with people, and I am accepting them just as they are.")*:

1.

2.

3.

4.

5.

Choose one of these affirmations. Write it down on a separate sheet of paper. Read it often.

STUDENT AFFIRMATION

PURPOSE

To build and strengthen positive self-concept through regular use of positive affirmations.

PROCEDURE

1. Review with students the value of using affirmations.

2. Every day for at least 1 week take a few minutes to have the class say the affirmation paragraph out loud together. Energy and enthusiasm is the key in saying it. Make it fun and light.

DISCUSSION

1. How do you feel after saying the affirmation paragraph?

2. Which of the options did you prefer the most? Why?

OPTIONS

1. Have different students lead the class in saying it each day.

2. Try creative ways of doing it.

- One student says one word and then it moves on to the next student who says one word, and so on.

- Sing it; create a melody with hand clapping or finger snapping to accompany the "affirmation" song.

- Have the boys call out one sentence, then the girls call out the next sentence and keep going.

- Change tempos or volume. Say it as a whisper or a cheer.

3. Have the class record it on an audio tape and sing along with it each day.

4. Students can pair off and have the partners read it to each other, substituting the third person pronouns (i.e., "You, Ben, are a great person and wonderful things are happening in your life!").

5. Have the class compose their own version of an affirmation paragraph and use that together regularly.

6. Suggest the class make a decorative poster of it and hang it up in the classroom.

7. Have them put it up in their room at home in a place where they will see and read it each day (i.e., on the mirror in the bathroom, on a wall in their bedroom, etc.).

STUDENT AFFIRMATION

By using affirmations, you strengthen your positive qualities. Affirmations are meant to be said out loud, sung or read silently. It is important to put a lot of emotion and enthusiasm into saying them. Use the "Student Affirmation" often. The more you think about it, say, sing or read it, the more solid and real it becomes.

"I, _____ (fill in your name), am a great person, and wonderful things are happening in my life! I am cooperating and enjoying my parents, family and friends each and every day. I am committing to myself and loving to learn. I am easily achieving my goals in school. My school work habits and cooperation are excellent. I enjoy sharing my positive attitude with myself and others. I am learning from my mistakes and am improving every day.

I am making the best of my life and the best of me. I deserve it!"

ADVERTISING ME

PURPOSE

1. To provide a structure for students to express their creativity.

2. To explore and share the uniqueness of each person.

3. To become aware of the reactions people have to "bragging" about themselves.

4. To build group cohesiveness.

PROCEDURE

1. See activity sheet for instructions.

2. Encourage creativity. Be appreciative of their efforts.

3. Be aware of students' reactions, especially discomfort, and their ways of handling these emotions.

    Note: You may see patterns here that are similar to behavior you've witnessed before. The insight into the purpose of the behavior (i.e., to cover discomfort) may assist you in working with your students more effectively.

4. Provide time and space to share ads.

DISCUSSION

1. Provide discussion time for students to explore and share their feelings as the project progresses.

2. Assist them in becoming aware of what they did with those feelings. Did it work for them and in the group?

OPTIONS

1. Allow time for students to look at each others' ads.

2. Have students write in their journals about the experience and to acknowledge themselves for their good work.

ADVERTISING ME

Make an advertisement or commercial (or both) to sell yourself. You may design magazine or newspaper advertisements, posters, billboard signs, brochures, radio or television commercials or any other form of advertising you choose. You might want to write a poem or a song that advertises who you are.

Use whatever materials are available to you:

Poster paper, crayons, markers, water colors, brushes, scissors, magazines, newspapers, digital images and paste. If available, you could use a laptop word document, voice recorder, camera - photos, videos etc.

Be prepared to share your ad with the class.

COME ON DOWN

PURPOSE

1. To express positive qualities publicly.

2. To have fun.

3. To build group support and cohesion.

PROCEDURE

1. Presented with "TV game show" excitement, "Come On Down" is a self-esteem version of a popular TV game show which involves contestants being told to "Come On Down". This game works best with a lot of enthusiasm and group support (applause). Refresh everyone on how thrilled people are on game shows when they are told to "Come On Down." Demonstrate or have a student demonstrate the thrill of racing to the front of the room in the "come on down" spirit.

2. Students either volunteer or are called on to "Come On Down". For example, "Eddie, Come On Down." The person runs up to the front, faces the class, and says their name and then completes the sentence "I'm the world's best _____." (This can be something they are good at, getting better at, or dream to be good at (i.e., "I'm the world's best dancer.").

3. The group gives that person a rousing applause as they run to the front, and as they finish their statement and return to their seat or the floor.

4. Repeat the activity with as many students as possible.

I AM GRATEFUL FOR

PURPOSE

1. To focus on gratitude.

2. To encourage awareness of the things in life for which you are grateful.

PROCEDURE

Students complete activity sheet.

I AM GRATEFUL FOR

Make a list of the people and things in your life for which you are grateful. Write ten or more ideas.

For example, I am grateful for:

   1. My mother
   2. My teacher
   3. My friends
   4. The ability to love other people
   5. My musical ability

I am grateful for:

1.

2.

3.

4.

5.

6.

7.

8.

9.

10.

GRATITUDE

PURPOSE

1. To heighten awareness of gratitude in life.

2. To encourage the expression of gratitude.

PROCEDURE

Students follow directions on activity sheet. Teacher might direct students as to whether this will be a partner or individual activity.

DISCUSSION

1. Is there more to be grateful for in your life than you anticipated?

2. How comfortable were you expressing your gratitude?

3. Do you usually focus on your gratitude?

GRATITUDE

This activity can be done with a partner, or you can do it by yourself using your journal. Answer the following questions. You may wish to go through the questions a number of times focusing on various people and things for which you are thankful or grateful.

1. For what are you grateful for?

Example, "I am grateful for my close friends."

2. Why are you grateful?

Example: "I feel grateful because we have a lot of fun together and we can be honest with one another."

3. How could you bring more of that into your life?

Example: "I could reach out to others more and make more new friends."

4. Who or what could you acknowledge more fully?

Example: "I could acknowledge my best friend, Sandy, and myself more fully for how we make our friendship special."

SUPER ME CAPE

PURPOSE

1. To build self-esteem.

2. To encourage giving statements of appreciation.

PROCEDURE

1. Each student is given a large rectangular "cape-sized" piece of butcher paper, a felt marker, and two pieces of masking tape.

2. On the top of their paper they print:

"_____, what's special about you is . . . "
       (their name)

3. The students assist one another in taping their capes onto their backs.

4. The students move about the room writing appreciative statements on the other people's capes.

5. After several minutes of milling and writing, everyone stops and takes off their capes. Each student takes turns reading aloud their "Super Me Capes" by declaring, "What's special about me is . . . ." Lots of class applause and support is offered as each person reads their cape.

DISCUSSION

1. Do we often take the time to say things like this to one another? Why or why not?

2. What feelings did you have when people were writing on your cape?

3. What feelings did you have when you read your statements aloud?

4. Did you have any trouble thinking of things to write? Why or why not?

OPTIONS

This activity can be structured to learn about famous people in history, current events, literature, etc.

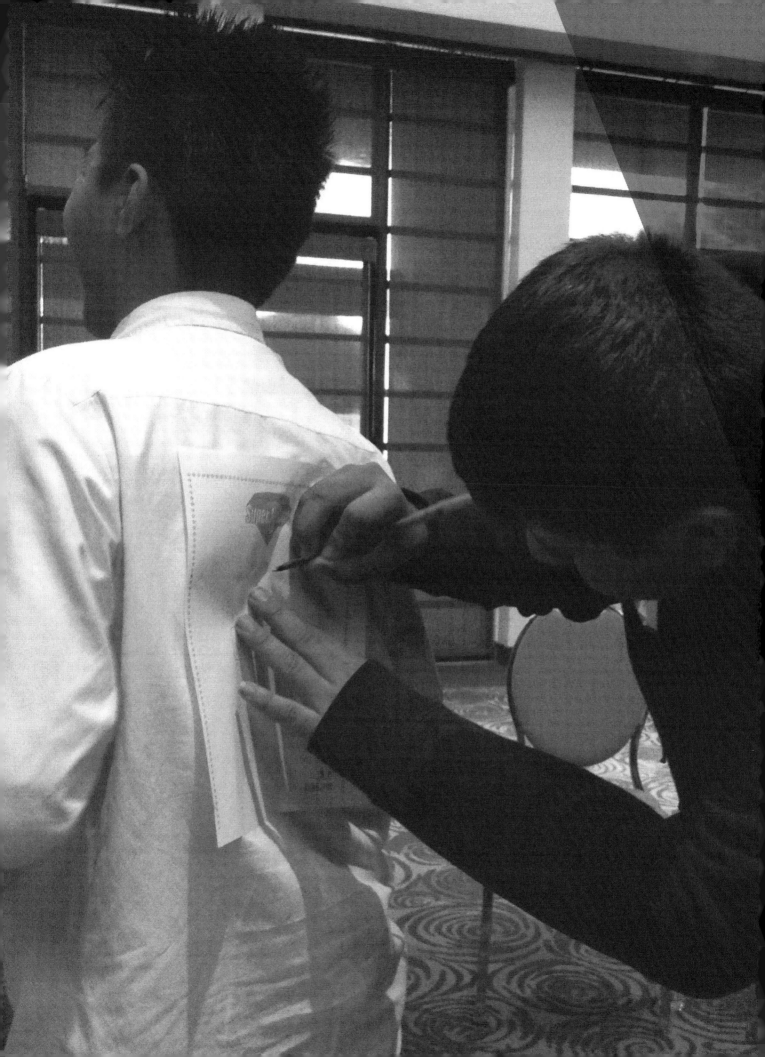

LETTER TO YOURSELF

PURPOSE

1. To encourage acknowledgment of self.

2. To receive the acknowledgment in the future and brighten the day.

PROCEDURE

Students complete activity sheet.

OPTIONS

1. Seal the letter in an envelope addressed to yourself. Mail it.

2. Give the sealed letter to a friend/teacher with a note asking them to mail it to you in a couple of weeks.

LETTER TO YOURSELF

Write a letter of caring support and encouragement to yourself. Imagine writing it with as much warmth as if you were writing it to the person you love the most in the entire world.

In your letter give yourself appreciation, wise advice, acknowledgment for the things you have done well, and forgiveness for the things you are still working on. Put your caring and understanding for yourself into the letter.

SUPER BOOSTER

PURPOSE

To practice giving and receiving positive support and appreciative feedback.

PROCEDURE

1. Students sit in arcs of five or six. Groups of students who feel comfortable together and know each other are suggested.

2. Each person heads a blank sheet of paper with their name and titles it "My Strengths" and then passes it to the person to their left.

3. Focusing on one person at a time (for 1-2 minutes), the entire group is to call out all the strengths and positive qualities they see in him/her. (i.e., "Marie, I like your sense of humor. I like your pretty eyes. I appreciate that you are my friend and that I can count on you...") The group shares what they like, admire, respect or appreciate. The person receiving the feedback remains silent and is encouraged to be open to listening to the "good news" while looking at the people giving the appreciative feedback.

The person to the left of the receiver is recording the strengths as they are being called out by the group in addition to calling out their own feedback.

The students are reminded that no "putdowns" are allowed– only positive statements. They are to look at the person to whom they are speaking.

The feedback statements are to be "I-statements" rather than "you-statements". For example, "I like your honesty," rather than, "You are honest." The first is sharing an experience while the second is more of a judgment and is less personally impactful. Using "I-statements" rather than "you" (evaluative or judgmental) statements is a powerful practice to use in future classroom activities.

4. Encourage the students to keep calling out the positive statements for the entire time and offer as much positive support as possible for the one receiving the feedback. Call time after 1-2 minutes and have the group give the first person applause.

5. Each person gets a turn receiving the group's strength feedback.

6. The recorders pass the "My Strengths" page back to the owner who reads the sheets and adds any additional strengths that may have been left out.

7. Each person then reads their list out loud, starting out with the words, "I am (or have) _____." (i.e., "I am humorous," "I have pretty eyes," etc.).

DISCUSSION

1. How did you feel giving positive feedback?
2. How did you feel receiving positive feedback?
3. Is one easier than the other? If so, why?
4. Did you believe what people told you? If not, why not?

CHAPTER 3
Creating Positive Relationships

TEACHING TIPS & SUGGESTIONS

1 Be open and available to deal with the range of feelings and reactions that may occur as students explore the sensitive issues of friendships. Allow the classroom to be a safe place for honest expression, even if it means disagreement, anger or hurt feelings. Let students know that sharing different points of view is encouraged. Encourage students to relate more openly with each other, and to trust expressing themselves more honestly. With caring support and understanding from you and other members of the class, students can move through their negative feelings with clarity and redirection.

2 Incorporate the communication and listening skills outlined in this chapter on a daily basis. The use of "I-statements" can be a helpful standard for everyone to use. Their use can replace common incidents of blaming and victimizing with a higher degree of personal accountability for feelings and behaviors.

3 Listen to what's behind your students' words. Encourage them as well to practice the skills of active and empathetic listening in interactions with each other.

4 Be watchful of any cliques or examples of exclusive behavior. Having students meet and work with a variety of new students in different ways can diminish the likelihood of "in" groups. Also, the cooperation games and Trust Circle activity can be used to assist in dealing with reoccurring exclusion.

ACTIVITY PREVIEWS

MAKING FRIENDS
Focus: Explore what's important in a friend and how to make friends.
Time: 50 minutes

POWER OF FRIENDSHIPS
Focus: Review the positive aspects of friendships.
Time: 30 minutes
Activity: Page III-08

FRIENDSHIP
Focus: Exploring personal belief systems.
Time: 15 minutes
Activity: Page III-11

WHAT'S MY FEELING?
Focus: Non-verbal communication of feelings.
Time: 20-30 minutes

KEEPING FRIENDS
Focus: Explore maintaining friendships through problem solving and role playing.
Time: 50 minutes

TRUSTING
Focus: Build an awareness of trust in self and others.
Time: 30 minutes
Activity: Page III-15

THE TIES THAT BIND
Focus: Discover how communication can enhance group cohesion.
Time: 15-20 minutes

TEAM TALE
Focus: Enhance communication skills through writing a class story.
Time: 20-30 minutes

TELEPHONE
Focus: Experience how communication through gossip can get distorted.
Time: 20 minutes

I'M LISTENING
Focus: Practice active listening while sharing ideas.
Time: 30 minutes

WHAT I HEARD YOU SAY WAS . . .
Focus: Enhance active listening skills while sharing personal views.
Time: 30-50 minutes

POINT OF VIEW
Focus: Becoming aware of different perceptions/points of view.
Time: 30 minutes
Activity: Page III-27

TALKING IT OUT: RESOLVING CONFLICT
Focus: One to one problem resolution.
Time: 20-40 minutes

TRUST CIRCLE
Focus: A supportive, caring communication activity.
Time: 2 class sessions initially, then varies.

EXPRESSING RESENTMENTS AND APPRECIATIONS
Focus: Develop an appropriate and responsible way to express feelings.
Time: 10 minutes

HEART–SEAT
Focus: Communicate with respect and caring while building group trust.
Time: 5 minutes per person in a group

BRAINSTORMING
Focus: Learning and practicing brainstorming skills.
Time: 2 sessions

TELL IT TO THE TEACHER
Focus: Build respect and trust between teacher and student.
Time: Varies

BUTTON PUSHING
Focus: Recognize what causes upset and what to do about it.
Time: 30 minutes

FORGIVING
Focus: Forgiving self and others.
Time: 10-20 minutes
Activity: Page III-41

COACHING PARTNERS
Focus: Peer coaching in a subject area.
Time: Varies

SURVIVAL
Focus: Build group participation through group problem solving.
Time: 40 minutes
Activity: Page III-46

MAKING A DIFFERENCE IN SOMEONE'S LIFE
Focus: Take action without controlling another's experience.
Time: 15-20 minutes
Activity: Page III-49

MAKING FRIENDS

PURPOSE

1. To increase awareness of what is important to look for in a friend.

2. To explore methods of making friends.

PROCEDURE

1. Lead a class discussion session on what makes a good friend (i.e., qualities, characteristics and behaviors).

2. Ask students to notice when they have the qualities they find important.

3. The class may want to prioritize their ideas from #1, most important to the least important. Remember there are no rights or wrongs.

4. Now have students break into groups of 4 or 5 and discuss methods of making friends. Ask each group to make a list of their ideas and star the two best or most effective ones.

5. Have a spokesman from each group share the list with the larger group.

6. Have each group role play their starred methods and share their role play with the class.

DISCUSSION

1. Do we often take the time to say things like this to one another? Why or why not?

2. What feelings did you have when people were writing on your cape?

3. What feelings did you have when you read your statements aloud?

4. Did you have any trouble thinking of things to write? Why or why not?

OPTIONS

Groups can also list ways that do not work in making friends and role play those, pointing out what doesn't work and then shifting the method so it might work.

POWER OF FRIENDSHIPS

PURPOSE

1. To become aware of the value of friendships.

2. To develop greater accountability for the quality of the friendships students build.

PROCEDURE

1. Have your students read about a celebrity they are familiar with who befriends kids and inspires them to excel.

2. Lead a discussion on the importance of friendships in their lives.

3. Have the students complete the activity sheets.

DISCUSSION

1. What makes a good friend?

2. What do you appreciate most about your friends?

3. What do you think they appreciate most about you?

4. What is your opinion about the "friendship level" for us as a class?

5. What can you do to build it even stronger?

OPTION

1. Instead of a written exercise, the questions can be done in partnership, small groups, or discussions.

2. Have students find articles in newspapers or magazines that demonstrate positive aspects of friendships. Have them bring them in to share or report on.

POWER OF FRIENDSHIPS

Friendships can be a very wonderful part of life. When you make your friendships special, you can get much in return. As you complete these sentences, honestly look at what friendships mean to you.

1. A friend to me is:

2. Things I like to do with my friends are:

3. Places I like to go with my friends are:

4. My best friends are:

5. Ways I can make friends are:

6. When I make a friend I feel:

7. When I lose a friend I feel:

8. Some ways I can make myself feel better, when I lose a friend, are:

9. Unfriendly things I sometimes do are:

10. Friendly things I do are:

11. Something I can change in my friendships is:

FRIENDSHIP

PURPOSE

1. To explore values and beliefs about friendship.

2. To heighten awareness of what you can do to be a better friend.

PROCEDURE

1. Discuss beliefs about friendships with students. Almost everyone likes to have friends and good friendships. However, sometimes we don't have the friends we want because of what we think and feel about ourselves and this stops us from making new friends.

> *Beliefs that limit friendship:*
> - I'm not good enough (I'm not worthy).
> - I'm too good.
> - I'd have to change myself.
> - I'm too shy.
> - I don't have money.
> - I might get hurt.
> - I can only have a few good friends.
> - They might misuse me.
> - They're different from me.
> - They don't/won't understand me.

If we think that friends won't be good for us, we will make sure we won't have many! The way to have more friendships and better relationships is to change what we think and feel about ourselves. We can start to think good things that assist us in making friends.

> *Beliefs that enhance friendships:*
> - I am enough! I am worthy of any friends that I want!
> - I am beautiful, and I also see the beauty in everyone around me.
> - I can be myself and have plenty of friends.
> - I am a sensitive and strong person.
> - I always have more than I need to get what I want.
> - I handle difficulties with ease and grace.
> - I have and choose as many friends as I want.
> - I cherish the uniqueness and value the specialness of others.
> - I communicate clearly.

2. Read or write these positive statements over and over with feeling and enthusiasm. If you think and feel this way about friends, you can have as many friends as you want! Have students say some or all of these statements. Ask them to write the five they like the most on a sheet in their journals.

3. Students complete activity sheet.

FRIENDSHIP

Fill in the blanks below:

What I believe about myself that stops me from having good friendships is:

1.

2.

3.

What makes me a good friend is:

1.

2.

3.

Things I can do to improve my friendships are:

1.

2.

3.

Choose and star one of the above improvements that you are willing to work on this week. Do it for one week and then complete the following:

What I learned about myself regarding my friendships is:

WHAT'S MY FEELING?

PURPOSE

1. To increase awareness about how feelings are communicated.

2. To enhance accurate perception of feelings.

PROCEDURE

1. Discuss how body language and tone of voice can be important keys to understanding the feeling behind a communication. Give examples of how these cues can help us to accurately interpret the meaning in what is being communicated. For example, when someone teases us, it may really convey affection, although the words themselves may not communicate that.

2. Have the class generate a list of feelings they experience and write these on the board. Complete the list with any emotions you feel are important that have not been volunteered.

3. Use a phrase such as, "That's wonderful" to demonstrate how it could be said to convey emotions such as enthusiasm, anger, disappointment, etc. Ask student volunteers to do the same in front of the class with other words or phrases and have the class guess what feeling is being portrayed.

4. Have student volunteers demonstrate non-verbally and ask the class to identify the feeling they think is being portrayed.

DISCUSSION

1. What are some ways feelings are demonstrated?

2. Have you ever misunderstood what someone was saying to you because you ignored or misinterpreted the feeling behind it?

3. Are some people better than others at communicating feelings? Is this an easy thing for you to do?

OPTIONS

1. Have students use only facial expressions to demonstrate feelings.

2. Have students non-verbally demonstrate the feelings conveyed by different pieces of music.

KEEPING FRIENDS

PURPOSE

1. To practice conflict-resolution skills as they pertain to friendships.

2. To enhance creative problem solving ability.

PROCEDURE

1. Have students sit in a circle. Ask students what sort of disagreements, disputes, or issues come up between friends - particularly ones that can hurt a friendship. Write these on the board.

2. Ask for volunteers to choose an issue and role play the disagreement. Freeze them when the point has been made and the energy is high.

3. Ask the group to brainstorm solutions.

4. Have the same volunteers quietly discuss which solution they will use and then role play it for the group.

DISCUSSION

1. Did the solution work? Why/Why not?

2. Can that solution be used in other situations?

3. Did you have to give anything up to resolve the issue (i.e., being right, pride)?

4. When you resolved the issue, what did you make more important than your opinion or pride?

5. Was there a difference in how you felt role playing the two parts (conflict vs. resolution)?

TRUSTING

PURPOSE

To build an awareness of self-trust and trust in others.

PROCEDURE

1. Have students answer the questions on the activity sheet.

2. Have students choose a partner and share their responses. Give them 5-10 minutes to do so. You can have students choose partner A & B and give them several minutes each to share or let them self-monitor their time with periodic reminders from you at three, five, seven, and ten minutes.

3. After they've shared, ask each partner to write on the back of their partner's activity sheet three ways they think their partner is trustworthy.

DISCUSSION

1. Were the questions difficult to answer? Why or why not?

2. What are the reasons you sometimes don't trust yourself? Others?

3. What ways did you think of to build trust? (list these)

4. Is trust important with teachers? Family? Friends? Why?

5. With which group is it most important to you? Why?

TRUSTING

Five reasons I trust myself are:

1.

2.

3.

4.

5.

Five people I trust are:

1.

2.

3.

4.

5.

I trust them because:

I think people trust me because:

I can earn my own and others' trust by:

THE TIES THAT BIND

PURPOSE

1. To enhance group cohesion.

2. To practice acknowledging self and others.

3. To practice communicating feelings.

PROCEDURE

1. Divide the class into groups of 8-10 students.

2. Ask students to think about something they are proud of or a positive quality they possess.

3. One student begins the process by sharing a positive statement about himself (i.e., "I am a good basketball player," or "I am determined and have a lot of enthusiasm.") He/she then holds the end of a ball of yarn while tossing the rest of the ball to another student in the circle. The process continues until everyone in the circle has had a turn.

DISCUSSION

1. What does this design you jointly created reflect to you?

2. What helps tie the group together?

PROCEDURE *(Continued)*

4. Ask students to think of a positive quality or something they like about other members in the group.

5. The person holding the ball of yarn begins by tossing the ball to someone in the circle and then making a positive statement about that person (i.e., "Fred, you're a great friend!"). That person continues the process until the ball is completely unravelled.

DISCUSSION *(Continued)*

3. How did you feel doing the process? What did you like about it?

4. Was it easier to compliment yourself or others?

5. How else can we "tie" our group together?

OPTIONS

1. Instead of yarn, use a ball which is tossed to the next speaker.

2. Use "value" questions such as:

> *"What irritates me about other people is . . . ."*
>
> *"What I like best about my family is . . . ."*
>
> *"What I have the hardest time dealing with is . . . ."*

TEAM TALE

PURPOSE

1. To help all students experience making a contribution to a class project.

2. To assist all students in feeling part of the classroom group.

PROCEDURE

1. The class forms a circle and is instructed that they will compose a story about their class that makes sense.

2. One student in the circle says the first sentence in the story, the next person adds the second sentence to the story, and so on, until a story is generated and a logical conclusion or place to stop is found. All students should be allowed to participate at least three times.

3. Any student may pass if he or she cannot think of a sentence. Active listening as each student speaks is emphasized.

DISCUSSION

1. Does the story you have made up describe the class? How? What important things about this class were left out?

2. Does this story describe how most of the students feel about this class? If not, why?

3. Would you recognize the class from hearing just the story?

OPTIONS

1. The story can be written down as it is developed. It then can be duplicated and given to each student or compiled in a class book.

2. Voice may be recorded instead of writing the story down. Stories can be developed on any topic about which you would like to get students' ideas/feelings.

3. Have small groups create their own stories.

TELEPHONE

PURPOSE

To allow students to notice how communication can be distorted and to experience the effects of distorted communication.

PROCEDURE

A group of 6 to 10 students sit together in a circle or a line. One student begins by whispering the designated sentence(s) in his neighbor's ear. The neighbor repeats it to the next person in line, and so on. When the whispered sentence(s) has/have gone to the last person, the final version is compared to the original.

DISCUSSION

1. What are the reasons that communication gets distorted? What happened with this?

    - Ambiguous information

    - Careless and/or selective listening

    - Intent to misrepresent someone *(put them down while building yourself up)*

2. Have students share examples of times when others distorted their communication and vice versa. How did it feel when that happened?

3. What are ways to prevent passing on information that is distorted?

    - Check it out with the original source

    - Refrain from talking "behind someone's back" (gossip)

    - Listen carefully

    - Ask people to repeat back what it is you told them so you know that they heard you correctly.

OPTIONS

1. Have five students volunteer and ask them to leave the room. The statement(s) is/are passed out or written on the board and then covered up so the class can follow along and notice what changes occur in the communication as it is passed from student to student. Have the first volunteer come back into the room and tell him/her the statement(s). Call the second volunteer and ask the first person to pass the message on to the second. Do this with all of the remaining volunteers. Ask the last person to give the final version to the whole class.

   Note: There can be a tendency to make fun of the volunteers as they make mistakes when repeating the story aloud. It's best to remind the class to listen carefully for any deletions or addition and to quietly support the volunteers.

2. Have the students generate possible statements prior to the beginning of the game.

3. Examples of statements that could be used are:

   "Gloria was in the back seat of the red convertible on the driver's side when we came to the flashing stoplight. We stopped and turned left, but a car ran the stop sign and came right toward where Gloria was sitting."

Both humorous statements and/or ones that relate to a certain subject can be used. For example, here are some that may be used for a history class:

   The inhabitants of ancient Egypt were called mummies. They lived in the Sarah Desert and traveled by Camelot.

   Another tale tells of William Tell, who shot an arrow through an apple while standing on his son's head.

   Columbus was a great navigator who discovered America while cruising about the Atlantic. His ships were called the Nina, the Pinto and the Santa Fe.

I'M LISTENING

PURPOSE

1. To practice active listening:

> - Use of silence
> - Non-verbal encouragement
> - Paraphrasing
> - Reflecting feelings

2. To share ideas and feelings about any given topic.

PROCEDURE

1. Discuss and demonstrate listening skills. To actively listen, the listener is focused on and attentive to the speaker. There is eye contact and no interruptions. The listener is concentrating on the speaker's words as well as the feelings behind the words. He/she is watching non-verbal expressions such as grimaces as well as acknowledging content. The active listener attempts to "walk in the speaker's shoes," to experience the world through the other's eyes and feelings without holding value judgments. Active listening requires full attention so the listener is not running his/her own agenda.

The elements of active listening to be practiced here are:

> **a) Attentiveness** - *Focus on the speaker, have eye contact and pay attention to what is being said.*
>
> **b) Suspend value judgments** - *Listen from the speaker's experience without judging what is being said as right or wrong.*
>
> **c) Non-verbal acknowledgment** - *Let the speaker know that you are listening with a nod, smile, uh-huh, or laugh as appropriate.*
>
> **d) Rephrasing** - *When the speaker is finished, summarize the main points of what you heard. "What I heard you say was...Right?"*
>
> **e) Acknowledge the feelings behind the words** - *Let the speaker know what your observations of his/her feelings were and how you felt hearing what was said ("It seemed to me that you felt sad when that happened. Did you? I felt sad just listening to you explain it.") Be sure to check out your observations and interpretations with the speaker for accuracy.*

2. Ask the students to designate each member as an A, B or C. Ask for a show of hands of all A's, B's and all C's for clarification.

3. Explain that each person will have an opportunity to play each role in his/her triad. Write the following on the blackboard:

	A	B	C
1st Time	Observer	Speaker	Listener
2nd Time	Speaker	Listener	Observer
3rd Time	Listener	Observer	Speaker

4. Give speakers a topic of your choice to speak on for three-five minutes. (Example: "The pros and cons of giving grades in school.")

5. The listener is to practice one or two (no more than two) elements of active listening.

6. Ask observers to pay attention to the interaction. Give the triad 3-5 minutes. Then have the observer give feedback to the listener. (Include what they saw the listener doing both verbally and non-verbally, and their observations of how the speaker responded. What did the listener do that worked particularly well? What did not work very well?)

7. Switch roles according to the chart.

8. Each time this activity is done, students can practice different elements of active listening.

DISCUSSION

1. What was it like being listened to in that way?

2. What was it like to actively listen?

3. What did observers see that was positive or negative?

4. What helps tie the group together?

WHAT I HEARD YOU SAY WAS

PURPOSE

1. To enhance listening skills.

2. To establish self-regulating skills amongst group members.

3. To share personal views and ideas.

4. To learn to consider another point of view before stating your own.

PROCEDURE

1. Review the tenets of active listening, particularly rephrasing, and seeing the world through the speaker's experiences without judgment.

2. Indicate to the students that part of the goal in this activity is to practice speaking with another, rather than at them.

3. Have students divide into groups of 4-8 and sit in a circle.

4. One person is chosen to start as the monitor. The other group members choose a topic which could be discussed from a social or personal viewpoint, such as the world, school, etc. and on which they all have a point of view. (The teacher may want to assign the first topic).

5. The person to the left of the monitor briefly states his/her point of view on the topic. Another person rephrases or summarizes the main idea of what person #1 said before starting his/her own views.

6. The monitor is the group's self-regulator. He/She stops any interrupting and reminds people if they don't rephrase.

7. The teacher periodically has the monitor switch roles with a group member.

8. Different topics of discussion can be chosen as needed throughout the activity to keep things going.

TOPIC - LEGALIZING DRUGS

Person 1: "I'm in favor of legalizing drugs because then there won't be so much money spent on the black market for drugs."

Person 2: "Okay. I heard you say that you favor legalizing drugs to get the money out of the black market. Right?"

Person 1: "Yep!"

Person 2: "I think legalizing drugs will just create more addicts . . ."

Person 3: "Yeah, but . . ."

Monitor: "Wait a minute Person 3. Are you aware that you interrupted? He wasn't finished yet, and you forgot to rephrase what he said."

Person 3: "Okay, sorry."

Person 2: continues . . .

DISCUSSION

1. Did you feel listened to in this activity?

2. Was it different for you than other conversations? How?

3. Did you find yourself listening better?

4. How can this skill affect your relationships?

POINT OF VIEW

PURPOSE

1. To promote an awareness of different points of view.

2. To demonstrate how one's point of view can effect communications.

PROCEDURE

1. Ask students to form groups of 4-8. Instruct them to turn to the young girl/old woman drawing and glance at it briefly, without discussion, then put their books aside.

2. Ask students to share what they saw in the picture with their group. Emphasize the concept that people perceive differently by asking questions such as, "Would you talk to this person on the bus?" or "In your family, of whom does this person remind you?"

3. Have them turn back to the picture and continue their discussion.

4. Assist people who have difficulty identifying both aspects of the drawing.

5. Expand discussions to other areas in which a person's point of view might be limited by his/her perception of information (parent/child, teacher/student, etc.)

DISCUSSION

1. Is there a "correct" way to see the picture? Did you think there was?

2. Is anyone able to see both aspects simultaneously?

3. Name some situations when you "knew" you were "right" and so did someone else, and both "rights" were different. How did you feel? What happened?

4. How might interpersonal conflicts result from individuals perceiving information differently? How might such conflicts be resolved?

5. What did you feel towards those who saw the drawing the same way you did? Towards those who saw it differently?

6. What did you feel when you "discovered" the other aspect of the picture?

7. How does this happen in the world?

8. What strategies can you use in your life to avoid point of view conflicts like these?

TALKING IT OUT: RESOLVING CONFLICT

PURPOSE

1. To demonstrate a method of resolving conflict by showing feelings.

2. To help students learn new ways of communicating.

3. To encourage awareness of feelings in self and in others.

PROCEDURE

1. Ask the class to sit in a circle.

2. Ask for volunteers of students who have a conflict that they have not resolved or choose a pair that you are aware of.

3. Ask the students to sit facing each other in the center of the circle.

4. Have the students describe the problem from their own points of view.

5. Next, ask each student to share what he or she is feeling about the situation, focusing on their experience not what the other is doing. Assist them to phrase their communication using "I-statements".

> *Example: "I feel hurt when you exclude me from the group," not, "You are mean to me and make me feel bad when you exclude me."*

6. Have each student repeat what they heard the other say. Repeat this until it is accurate to the other person.

7. Ask each for an action step to help resolve the situation. (Ask the class for suggestions if they are stuck.)

8. Have them share words of appreciation to one another for being open and honest while listening to the other's point of view.

DISCUSSION

1. What is the effect of communication with "I-statements"?

2. What is the value of confronting a conflict situation?

3. What did you learn as observers? As participants?

4. Can people share their feelings honestly without blaming others? How did you learn to do this?

OPTIONS

1. Have students share how they think the other person feels about the situation instead of sharing their own feelings. Have them get feedback from the other person as to the accuracy of their statements.

2. Have the students role play a new way of dealing with the conflict situation. *(i.e., role play the various possible solutions that the students/class discussed.)*

TRUST CIRCLE
(AKA "HEART TALKS")

PURPOSE

1. To introduce a tool for effective and caring communication.

2. To promote awareness of the importance of a safe place to share.

3. To build group cohesiveness, trust and support.

PROCEDURE

1. Discuss with the class times when they felt safe confiding in someone they could trust. Also discuss times when others confided in them. (Use your personal examples.) Review how valuable it can be for the class to create a "safe place" within their group for talking about things in a deeper, more honest way. Indicate that this activity is about creating a caring and safe place for sharing from that deeper, more "real" place from inside each of us.

2. Review the guidelines for leading a Trust Circle:

   a) One person speaks at a time. Everyone else listens without comments, side-talking, or interruptions.

   b) When the first person is done, the next person (either to the right or to the left) begins.

   c) Everyone is encouraged to blend honesty and personal responsibility in their sharing. Rather than statements of blaming others, students are to practice using "I" - statements.

   d) Everything that is said is kept confidential in the group.

   e) Though everyone is encouraged to talk, it is okay for someone to pass when it gets to be their turn in the circle.

   f) The speaker is encouraged to make eye contact with others in the group. The group supports each person by just listening.

   g) Everyone's comments are accepted. There is no need for anyone to contest or rebut someone's point of view.

3. Indicate that everyone, including you, will need to keep the agreements in order for it to be a safe place. If anyone forgets, they will be gently reminded by the teacher or a selected monitor.

4. Ask for a show of hands of those who agree to keep the guidelines. Be sure to raise your hand as well. Clarify with anyone who has any questions or concerns about the guidelines.

5. Have the students arrange their chairs in a circle. It is best to set aside all desks and tables. (Later, after students are familiar with this technique they can form small trust circles.)

6. Indicate the first topic. It is helpful if it is not too threatening, and most students will have some thoughts on it. It is fine for you to go first. Be willing to be vulnerable and risk. You can set the tone for the Trust Circle.

Example:

> "What is your favorite sport or hobby and why?"
>
> "What is something you wish adults would do differently?"
>
> "What was your most embarrassing moment?"

7. Begin the Trust Circle with someone who volunteers to start.

Possible topics for Trust Circles are:

- Who do you appreciate the most in your life and why?
- If you could change one thing about yourself, what would it be and why?
- Describe a time when you did something courageous/kind.
- How would you want the world to be different for your children?
- How do you "push" your parents' buttons?
- Describe a time you lied to get what you wanted.
- If your friend was going to describe all the great things about you, what would he/she say?
- What qualities do you look for in a friend?
- If you could teach everyone in the world one thing, what would it be?

DISCUSSION

Discuss the merits of this type of communication. Remind students that it is not a time to teach or get information, but a time to share in a safe and relaxed atmosphere.

EXPRESSING RESENTMENTS AND APPRECIATION

PURPOSE

1. To teach "I-statements".

2. To develop responsibility for one's feelings.

3. To learn appropriate ways to express feelings.

PROCEDURE

1. Set aside five to ten minutes regularly for this activity.

2. Define terms:

   a) **Resentment:** negative feelings concerning something that happened

   b) **Appreciation:** positive and grateful feelings concerning a person or an event

3. Teach "I-statements" for expressing either negative or positive feelings.

   Write these examples on the blackboard:

   Resentment: "I felt (name the feeling) when (name the person, behavior or event)."
   Example: "I felt angry when I got a low grade on the test."

   or

   "(Person's name) you made me (feeling) when (behavior or event)."
   Example: "You made me angry when you gave me a low grade on the test."

Discuss the differences between these two statements. The first has the speaker take responsibility for his/her own feelings, while the latter is a blaming statement. Allow the students to voice their concerns *(i.e., ". . . but you were the one who gave the grade." "Of course, but who took the test?")* assisting them in taking responsibility for their feelings.

4. Now move on to appreciation. Write this example on the blackboard:

   Appreciation: "I appreciate (name of person) for (name of event)."
   Example: "I appreciate (you), Ann, for driving me home from school yesterday."

As students begin to say these, they may feel awkward. It's okay. The awkwardness passes with practice.

5. Ask for volunteers who want to express an appreciation or resentment. Nothing has to be done with these feelings. The expression of them is what is most important. Be sure to follow-up with a student privately if any statements of resentment are expressions of serious concern. Follow-up general statements concerning the whole class with the full group. Be sure to ask the student if he/she wants assistance in solving a problem. The class can use problem-solving skills to assist if desired.

DISCUSSION

1. How do you feel now that you were able to say what you felt?

2. How was it for you to listen to others? (Hurt feelings may need some addressing here.)

HEART-SEAT

PURPOSE

1. To give each person an opportunity to talk honestly, respectfully, and with caring to each member of the group.

2. To let each person's words be heard.

3. To practice listening.

4. To build group trust.

PROCEDURE

1. Divide the class into small groups (6-8 students).

2. Ask who wants to go first and have them sit in a chair which will be designated the "Heart-Seat." The only job of the person in the "Heart-Seat" is to listen and receive feedback.

3. The group members take turns giving feedback by completing the first sentence.

4. After each member has taken a turn giving feedback, go around the circle again and complete the second sentence, then the third, etc., until all the sentences have been completed by every member.

5. Then it is another member's turn to sit in the "Heart-Seat" and receive the caring communication. Repeat this process until everyone has had their turn.

   Sentences to complete: (post these on the board)

   1. What I like or appreciate about you is . . . .
   2. What I would like more of from you is . . . .
   3. One thing that I could give more of to you is . . . .
   4. One thing I think you offer to this class is . . . .
   5. One thing that I want to thank you for is . . . .

6. Other possible sentences are:

   1. What I respect about you is . . . .
   2. The way I think I could be more helpful to you is . . . .
   3. What I notice about you that I like is . . . .
   4. Or make up some of your own!

7. Tell the students:

   • When you are in the "Heart - Seat," just listen without answering back or making comments.
   • Make eye contact as you both deliver and receive your communications.
   • Practice blending honesty and caring in your communication.
   • Have fun and allow the specialness of your group to build.

BRAINSTORMING

PURPOSE

1. To teach/practice the skill of brainstorming.

2. To build group cohesion.

3. To promote the application of brainstorming skills for problem-solving and information-gathering needs.

PROCEDURE

1. Ask students to call out, and you will write on the board, every idea they can think of, feasible or not, on the subject "Ways to Get Out of Doing School Work." Tell them they will have three minutes. No holds barred, be completely creative.

2. Ask students to comment on the activity. Was it fun? Did their ideas get outrageous? Did they add to others' ideas? Were they creative?

3. Tell students they have just utilized the skill of brainstorming. It is one of the most useful techniques available to solve a problem, gather information, and generate ideas. The idea in brainstorming is to produce as many ideas as possible, without assessing any of them, in a limited period of time. There are several guidelines that are important to follow for a successful brainstorming session.

4. Go over these with the students. Discuss the importance of each one.

>   a) Go for quantity - the more ideas the better.
>   b) Accept all ideas without judgment or comment of any kind.
>   c) Write or record every idea.
>   d) Offbeat, silly, outrageous, half-formed ideas are welcome and encouraged.
>   e) Piggyback on others' ideas.
>   f) Set a brief time limit (rarely as much as ten minutes) and stick to it.

QUANTITY is important because it adds the component of attempting to create as many ideas as possible. Quality ideas are more apt to come from a long list than a short one. It makes the activity into a game and helps to avoid censoring of ideas.

ACCEPTING all ideas without judgment is a cornerstone to this activity. It allows students to speak without fear of ridicule. It allows the creative process to flow. A workable idea often comes from what originally sounds silly. Additionally, a workable idea is often right under the unfeasible one in the creative process.

WRITING OR RECORDING EVERY IDEA is important to reinforce the atmosphere of acceptance. This is not a time to censor or evaluate ideas, only to generate them.

OFFBEAT, SILLY, HALF-FORMED IDEAS are welcomed and encouraged to enhance the students' creativity. An unusual idea may work. A partial thought may be completed by someone else.

PIGGYBACKING IDEAS is adding onto or expanding on someone else's idea. Working together cooperatively is more likely to solve a problem than working against one another. It is a compliment to have someone elaborate on your idea. This guideline creates a win-win environment.

SETTING A TIME LIMIT, and a brief one, channels the creative energy into generating ideas and away from wondering if there are enough ideas and how long will this go on. The activity remains focused. The timekeeper cuts in and stops the activity when time is up. A thirty second to one minute extension is okay if agreed upon by the group. Don't worry about lost ideas, they will come out later.

5. Do another warm-up activity, this time in small groups. Divide the class into groups of 4-6 students each. Give each student a slip of paper (or let them blindly choose) with one of the following topics written on it. Each group choses a timekeeper and a recorder. You say "GO" and the group has 3 minutes to generate as many ideas as possible on their topic. Students practice following the brainstorming guidelines.

   Topics:

   1. Ways to improve a shower.
   2. Uses for a pencil.
   3. Things to do while waiting in the doctor's office.
   4. Jobs for Batman.
   5. Things to program a robot to do.
   6. What to do when you rip the seat of your pants or dress at an important party.
   7. Ways to capture a wild elephant.
   8. Ways to communicate with an alien.

6. Have each group go through their list and circle all the feasible ideas. Now have them write a paragraph on the ideal scenario for their topic (i.e., best jobs for Batman, ideal uses for a pencil . . .)

7. Have groups share their lists and their paragraphs.

DISCUSSION

1. What was the process like for you?

2. Is thinking in this way fun?

3. Did you participate? If not, what held you back? Discuss these concerns.

4. Did lots of people in your group participate?

5. Were your group's ideas unusual?

6. In what ways could this technique help in your studies? In solving community and world dilemmas?

OPTIONS

Give students a choice of several realistic problems to brainstorm solutions for in their groups or in the large group - reducing pollution, regulating nuclear weaponry, gang warfare, drugs, dating issues, studying problems, etc.

After the brainstorming, ask the students to individually (or as a small group) develop several ideas into realistic and feasible solutions to the problem. Together assess if these ideas could be sent to community leaders - perhaps compiled into a report of possible solutions.

Emphasize the value that the long list of ideas and accepting format of brainstorming encourages. This list can later be honed down, reorganized and reworked to accomplish the task at hand.

TELL IT TO THE TEACHER

PURPOSE

1. To build trust and rapport between teacher and students.

2. To enhance communication skills.

3. To promote risk-taking and expressing feelings and perceptions.

PROCEDURE

Tell the students that it is important to feel that they can give you honest feedback about the way they experience your behavior and attitude toward them. It is helpful for you to know how your actions are viewed and interpreted by them. Below are several options on how to do this. The environment here is important. Just as they have been learning to do with each other, mention that you, too, are open to receiving feedback when it is delivered in an honest and caring way.

1. By Anonymous: Have the students write what they like and dislike about you, the classroom environment, their studies, the rules, etc. Someone collects them and gives them to you. No names are written on them.

2. Building Character: Write the following on the chalkboard:

"I feel (your name) is _____. I feel _____ when he/she (does what)." Have the students first write their answers down. Then ask them to read their answers while you record them on the board. Ask for clarification when you don't understand what the student has said. Ask for specific examples of your behavior. When this is completed, if there are things that you wish to change, ask the class to brainstorm ways of behaving to produce the result you want.

3. Mailbox: Have a different box in your classroom where students can write to you. Answer all the letters that are signed.

4. Progress Report: At the end of a grading period, distribute to each student a blank report card. Ask the students to grade you, commenting on your attitude, effort and offering suggestions for changes. Follow through by trying some of their suggestions.

5. Down-Load: Tell the students they will have three minutes to download all the resentments, angers and upsets they have about you and your class. You can have them do this on paper or call it out while you quickly (not neatly) write them on the board. Thank them for their honesty. This takes courage on your part. It can create a trusting atmosphere in the class while demonstrating risk-taking.

BUTTON PUSHING

PURPOSE

1. To recognize what upsets one another.

2. To find ways to work together to avoid dispute-causing situations.

3. To build group cooperation.

PROCEDURE

1. Ask students what "pushes their buttons" or gets them upset. Have them indicate if there is a particular place this occurs most (i.e., cafeteria line, classroom, hallway, home). Make a list of these on the board.

2. Have students partner up and sit across from their partner. Pick A & B.

3. B's go first. A's listen attentively. He/She chooses a "button" from the board and states (you may want to post or xerox these):

    a) My button is . . . (describes briefly and specifically).

    b) The way I handle this now is . . . (I get angry, I throw things, etc.)

    c) I will assist myself by . . . (new method handling situation, communication, walking away).

4. Give partner B 3-5 minutes to cycle through as many buttons as possible. Then instruct partner A's to begin, while B's listen.

5. Give partner A 3-5 minutes.

DISCUSSION

In the large group ask students what they found they could do to change their buttons being pushed. List them. Who is responsible for the button being a button? These lists may be valuable to post or hand out for reminders.

FORGIVING

PURPOSE

To forgive self and others.

PROCEDURE

Students complete activity sheet.

DISCUSSION

Students may want to share their answers. Ask students to share their experience of the exercise. Was it easy or hard to forgive? What feelings did you experience as you wrote? Spend time discussing the various feelings and thoughts they have about forgiving others. What if forgiving other people has nothing to do with whether the others were right or wrong? How can forgiveness make a difference in your relationship with others? What if forgiveness truly benefits the person who is doing the forgiving?

FORGIVING

Forgiveness of self and others is a very powerful process.

Complete the following statements:

I forgive myself for:

1.
2.
3.
4.
5.

I forgive _____ for:
(fill in name)

1.
2.
3.
4.
5.

I forgive myself for:

1.
2.
3.
4.
5.

I forgive _____ for:
(fill in name)

1.
2.
3.
4.
5.

I forgive myself for:

1.
2.
3.
4.
5.

I forgive _____ for:
(fill in name)

1.
2.
3.
4.
5.

COACHING PARTNERS

PURPOSE

1. To encourage cooperative learning.

2. To provide peer support for learning.

3. To assist students in understanding subject matter better.

PROCEDURE

1. Ask for volunteers in the class who feel confident in their understanding of a particular concept, principle, or subject.

2. Ask if these people would be willing to team up with students who are not yet sure of the material and provide "coaching."

3. Have students form equal size groups with at least one coach in each group.

4. Set a time period for this process and inform them that the goal is to have the students being coached be able to explain or demonstrate what they learned to their group at the end of the time.

5. Have students share their learnings with their group or with the class.

DISCUSSION

1. What was helpful to you in this process?

2. Were the coaches patient in explaining things?

3. Were there good listening skills on both sides? What facilitated this?

4. What did you learn that you could use to assist you in studying something else?

5. Did the coaches learn anything? What?

SURVIVAL

PURPOSE

1. To promote understanding of steps to be taken in providing more inclusion of self and others.

2. Build group cohesiveness.

PROCEDURE

1. Divide students into groups of 6-8.

2. Shuffle stacks of pre-made situation cards and resource cards. Have each group pick one situation card and five resource cards.

3. Students have ten minutes to rescue the group in their situation. They have only the five resources on their cards available to them.

4. Stop the groups after ten minutes and have each one report on their resources, situation, and rescue plan.

5. Hand out "Survey #1." Ask each student to respond anonymously and return it to you. Calculate the class' total of students who felt included and those who felt left out. Post these numbers on the board.

6. Repeat steps 2-4 with new cards for each group. Remind students to see if they can improve their class "felt included" tally.

7. Hand out "Survey #2." Calculate the new tallies and post.

DISCUSSION

1. Did the tally increase for those feeling included? Why?

2. What did you do to include yourself and others more the second time?

3. What does it feel like when you are not included?

4. Do people who feel included like their group more than people who do not feel included?

5. Is the group more effective when everyone feels included? Why or why not?

6. Do you ever feel like you are not included in other kinds of classroom groups?

7. What can you do this week to help more people feel included?

GROUP SITUATION CARDS

- Our car runs out of gas in the desert.
- Our group is caught in a snowstorm while hiking in the mountains.
- Our group is accidentally locked in the museum after hours.
- During an earthquake, our group is caught in an elevator between floors.
- Our van breaks down in a small village in the Soviet Union, where no one speaks English.
- Our boat washes ashore on a small, uninhabited island.
- Our group becomes separated from the large group while on a safari in Africa.
- Our group is accidentally locked in an abandoned warehouse.

RESOURCE CARDS

Compass	Digital camera	Magazine
Aluminum foil	Four quarters	Marking pens
Fishing line	Kitchen matches	Candles
Cell phone	Bicycle	Bottle of Coke
Rubber bands	Basketball	Parachute
German Shepherd	Tablet	Lantern
10 feet of rope	Coconut	Smart watch
Adhesive tape	Hatchet	Trumpet
Hammer & 12 nails	Pillowcase	Box of paper clips
Sack of walnuts	Laptop	

SURVIVAL

SURVEY #1

Answer these questions honestly. Do not put your name on the page.

Did you feel you were a part of your group, or did you feel left out?

Check One:

    _____ I felt part of my group.

    _____ I felt left out.

To feel more included in my group I could:

SURVEY #2

Answer these questions honestly. Do not put your name on the page.

Check One:

    _____ I felt part of my group.

    _____ I felt left out.

Circle One:

    I felt **more / less** a part of my group than last time.

What I did differently to feel more included was:

    _____ It worked.

    _____ I t didn't work.

MAKING A DIFFERENCE IN SOMEONE'S LIFE

PURPOSE

1. To discover ways to make a difference in others' lives.

2. To introduce the concept that each one of us chooses our own feelings.

PROCEDURE

See activity sheet for instructions.

DISCUSSION

1. Discuss the differences in attitude, feelings, and results between "making someone feel good" and "contributing to someone's state of mind and allowing them to choose their own emotions."

2. Can anyone, in fact, really make someone feel good or bad? Who is in charge of your feelings?

3. In what ways do we depend on others to "make us feel good" or blame them for "making us feel bad?"

MAKING A DIFFERENCE IN SOMEONE'S LIFE

Each person is responsible for his own feelings. No one can make another feel good or bad. However, we can contribute to a person in ways that might make it easier for them to feel more positive.

> *Example: Someone has just failed an important test. If we walk up and say, "Hey, stupid, any dummy could've passed that one," we are probably not contributing much to that person changing his mood. If, instead we were to say encouraging things, it might make it easier for that person to choose to feel better.*

Below are 10 ways to contribute to others. Add 10 more at the bottom of the list. See if you can do at least 3 of the items on the list of 20, today.

1. Apologize to someone you may have offended.
2. Send someone a card that says, "I care about you."
3. Ask if you can help someone.
4. Plan a surprise for someone.
5. Say hello to someone you don't know.
6. Ask someone who speaks a different language to teach you a word.
7. Do some shopping, go to the store, or do a favor for someone.
8. Clean up an area that needs straightening up.
9. Thank someone for being a friend.
10. Include someone who is left out.

11.

12.

13.

14.

15.

16.

17.

18.

19.

20.

CHAPTER 4
Personal Response-ability

TEACHING TIPS & SUGGESTIONS

1 Use the principles of this chapter as they relate to daily occurrences in the classroom. Typical events can lead directly to practicing the skills of choosing attitude, risking, keeping agreements, and taking personal responsibility for one's own feelings. The process of being together and working in the class can serve as the laboratory for what students are learning. The suggested attitude, rather than making anyone wrong for not practicing the skills covered, is one of providing insightful reminders for improvement.

2 Create opportunities, at times, for the class to choose the activities they are going to do on a certain day. By giving them that authority, you allow them to take greater charge of expressing their positive "abilities to respond" (response-ability).

ACTIVITY PREVIEWS

CARING FOR YOURSELF
Focus: Find ways to better care for yourself.
Time: 10 minutes
Activity: Page IV-05

TAKING CARE OF YOURSELF AND HELPING OTHERS
Focus: Examining behavior around care for self and others.
Time: 30 minutes
Activity: Page IV-07

GAMES PEOPLE PLAY
Focus: Through an activity and discussion, students explore limiting behavior.
Time: 20 minutes
Activity: Page IV-09

EXAMINING ATTITUDES
Focus: The role of attitudes in the achievement of success.
Time: 15 minutes
Activity: Page IV-12

HAVE TO/CHOOSE TO
Focus: Group milling activity to explore choice in attitude.
Time: 20 minutes

IMPOSSIBLE? MAYBE NOT!
Focus: Partner activity demonstrating changing the words we use in order to take more responsibility in our lives.
Time: 20 minutes

CHANGING ATTITUDES
Focus: Students acknowledge times they've changed their attitudes and identify ones they'd like to change.
Time: 15 minutes
Activity: Page IV-20

LEARNING FROM MISTAKES
Focus: Exploring attitudes about mistakes.
Time: 15 minutes
Activity: Page IV-23

MOCK ARGUMENT
Focus: A staged argument leads to learning about points of view and assumptions.
Time: 20 minutes

ARE YOUR FEELINGS DRIVING YOU?
Focus: Explore how to deal with feelings.
Time: 30 minutes
Activity: Page IV-28

LETTING GO OF JUDGMENT AND GUILT
Focus: Keys to eliminate guilt and minimize the "shoulds" we place against ourselves.
Time: 20-30 minutes
Activity: Page IV-32

LETTING GO OF RESENTMENT
Focus: Keys to letting go of resentment and building acceptance.
Time: 20-30 minutes
Activity: Page IV-36

RISK EXERCISE
Focus: Heighten awareness of risk-taking behavior through participation.
Time: 20 minutes

I SCARE MYSELF
Focus: Partnering activity exploring fear and how to take charge of emotions.
Time: 30 minutes

MEET THE PRESS
Focus: Take moderate risks in a supportive environment.
Time: 15 minutes

TAKE A STAND
Focus: Communication of preferences and points of view.
Time: 10-30 minutes

I AGREE/I DISAGREE
Focus: Nonverbal activity encouraging active and spontaneous decision-making.
Time: 15 minutes

CAN I QUOTE YOU ON THAT
Focus: The wisdom of others serves as a reflection of personal values.
Time: 15-30 minutes

VIEWPOINTS IN THE ROUND
Focus: Learn to express views and see issues from different points of view.
Times: 30 minutes

BROKEN AGREEMENTS
Focus: Reflective written activity exploring the personal benefits received for keeping our word with ourselves and others.
Time: 20-30 minutes
Activity: Page IV-52

TAKING CHARGE
Focus: Examine the level of self-responsibility students take in daily life.
Time: 10 minutes
Activity: Page IV-55

CARING FOR YOURSELF

PURPOSE

1. To identify ways to take care of yourself.

2. To commit to doing two of the identified ways.

PROCEDURE

Students complete the activity sheet.

DISCUSSION

During the week after introducing the activity, have the class discuss their experiences of completing their two choices.

1. How can you make self-care a habit?

2. When you take care of yourself, how can that positively affect others?

3. What is meant by the statement: "Take care of yourself, so you can take care of others."?

CARING FOR YOURSELF

Make a list of the ways you can take better care of yourself.

For example, I can take better care of myself by:

    1. Saying more positive things to myself.
    2. Eating more healthy foods and exercising more.
    3. Getting more sleep on weekday nights.
    4. Keeping my word with myself and others.
    5. Going to the movies with my favorite friends.

I can take better care of myself by:

1.

2.

3.

4.

5.

6.

7.

8.

9.

10.

Check two of the items on your list that you are willing to do this week. Do them this week and enjoy the results.

MAKING THE BEST OF ME | **CHAPTER 4: IV-05**

TAKING CARE OF YOURSELF AND HELPING OTHERS

PURPOSE

1. To become aware of how students are taking care of themselves and helping others.

2. To examine the feelings involved in these actions.

3. To explore the blocks or limitations to these actions.

PROCEDURE

1. Have each student complete the activity sheet.

2. This activity can be used at different points in the semester so the students can become aware of changes.

DISCUSSION

Discuss each question. Explore feelings and what the students might do to go beyond whatever stops them from taking care of self or others.

- Why is it important?

- Which is easier, taking care of self or assisting others?

- How far should you go in assisting others (re: drugs, gangs)?

- How much responsibility do you have in assisting a friend? a family member? a stranger?

- When might it be wise not to assist another?

- What is the difference between helping (doing for someone) and assisting (working with them so they can help themselves)? Which is more effective?

TAKING CARE OF YOURSELF AND HELPING OTHERS

1. Some of the ways I take care of myself are:

2. Some of the ways I have helped others are:

3. When I take care of myself, I feel:

4. When I help others, I feel:

5. When I help others, they respond by:

6. What do you think stops people from assisting others?

7. What sometimes stops you?

8. What do you want to do about that?

MAKING THE BEST OF ME | **CHAPTER 4: IV-07**

GAMES PEOPLE PLAY

PURPOSE

1. To increase awareness of limiting behaviors ("games").

2. To generate ideas of more positive ways to get what you want.

PROCEDURE

1. Define terms.

> **Games:** *The ways you act that limit you or hold you back from being all you can be (acting bored, tough, cool . . .)*
>
> **Payoffs:** *What benefits do we seem to get out of our behavior that we want or think we want (popularity, show someone up, get out of doing something, pity, attention, . . .)*

2. Have students complete the activity sheet.

DISCUSSION

1. What are the "games" you play?

2. What are the payoffs?

3. Did you find that the payoffs were the same or different from what you really want?

4. Do you think the payoffs will be any different if you try new behaviors?

5. How does your attitude affect whether or not you play your "games" to get what you want?

OPTIONS

1. Have students discuss in small groups.

2. Use the questions on the activity sheet as the basis for a partnership exercise.

GAMES PEOPLE PLAY

Complete the following statements:

1. The "games" (or ways I act) that limit me or hold me back are:

    (Examples: acting cool, shy, tough, bored, etc.)

2. The "payoffs" for (or what I get out of) playing these games are:

    (Examples: showing someone up, getting out of doing something, etc.)

3. What I really want is:

4. To get that, instead of playing my "games" I can:

    (Examples: be honest, take more risks, be more considerate, participate more, etc.)

EXAMINING ATTITUDES

PURPOSE

1. To identify positive and negative attitudes.

2. To examine how we perpetuate negative attitudes.

3. To explore how negative attitudes may keep us from achieving success.

PROCEDURE

1. Define positive and negative attitudes with the students. We have positive attitudes about things we are attracted to or find interesting. We may have negative attitudes about things we want to stay away from or tell ourselves we don't like.

An attitude all by itself is not positive or negative. Positive attitudes are not good and negative ones are not bad. It only makes a difference when we decide to do something, to achieve a goal. With a goal in mind, we must examine whether our attitudes will lead us toward success or away from it. Then we can determine if we want to change the attitude or not. Often it is our own negative self-talk that keeps a negative attitude going.

2. Have students complete the activity sheet.

3. In small groups, partnerships, or in the large group, students share their answers for questions 2 & 3.

DISCUSSION

1. Students share their positive/negative attitudes.

2. Brainstorm with the group how they could begin to change their attitudes.

3. Lead a discussion about the 'payoffs' for their negative attitudes (see Games People Play for definition of payoffs). How do these negative attitudes serve them?

EXAMINING ATTITUDES

1. We have positive attitudes about things we lean towards or are attracted to. Thinking about people, things, ideas, places, or situations, complete each of the following with three things you have positive attitudes about.

Example: "I like history."

Now do the same for negative attitudes. Those are the things you lean away from.

I like:

1.

2.

3.

I don't like:

1.

2.

3.

I want to:

1.

2.

3.

I have to:

1.

2.

3.

I can:

1.

2.

3.

I can't:

1.

2.

3.

2. What limiting attitudes do you have that may be keeping you from your goals? Fill in the chart.

LIMITING ATTITUDE	GOALS IT MAY KEEP ME FROM ACHIEVING
For example: a) I don't like homework	a) Getting good grades
b) I can't talk to new people	b) Making a lot of new friends

1.

2.

3.

4.

5.

3. What type of negative self-talk are you repeating to yourself that maintain these limiting attitudes and beliefs?

For example: "I am not as smart as others."
"Teachers give us too much work."
"I am too shy."

1.

2.

3.

4.

5.

HAVE TO / CHOOSE TO

PURPOSE

1. To explore the feelings created by the attitudes of "have to" and "want to".

2. To build awareness of individual choice regarding attitude.

PROCEDURE

1. Ask students: "Are there things in your life that you seem to HAVE TO do that you don't like doing?" (A HAVE TO is something we actually do, yet don't like doing.)

2. On the board, list their responses along with the feelings generated by those HAVE TOS.

I HAVE TO   **CREATE FEELINGS OF**

When list is complete ask: Are these feelings positive or negative?

3. Have students mill (walk) around the room, greet each other and say: "One thing I HAVE TO do is _____ and it's _____ fault." Tell students to exchange statements with as many classmates as possible. They can change their HAVE TO as many times as necessary. Tell them to use their bodies and exaggerate their feelings about that HAVE TO. It is a good idea to model this with a few students before they start. Give students 3 or 4 minutes.

4. Ask students: "How did it feel to do that?" "Who is really in charge of your feelings (mom, dad, teacher, you)?"

"What would be the opposite of 'HAVE TOS?" "WANT TOS." Ask students, "What are some of the WANT TOS in your life? Things you do because you want to." List these on the board:

WANT TOS   CREATE FEELINGS OF

When the list is complete ask: "Are these feelings positive or negative?"

5. Ask "Are 'WANT TOS' choices?" "Are 'HAVE TOS' choices?" Have students look closely at that. Emphasize the point (through questioning students) that we really don't HAVE TO do anything. We generally weigh the consequences - negative and positive and determine to do something or not.

The difference between 'HAVE TO' and 'WANT TO' is attitude.

CHOICE
→ **WANT TO** *(positive attitude)*
→ **HAVE TO** *(negative attitude)*

What makes us choose HAVE TO- blame, right/wrong, fear of risking . . .?

What if you chose a WANT TO attitude instead and still did the same things you would have done with a HAVE TO attitude before? Life might be more fun!!!

6. How do you do that?

   a) Realize you have a choice in your attitude.

   b) See your reward (internal or external) for doing the task.

Have students call out some rewards for doing those things they've been calling "have tos."

7. Have students do another mill with this statement:

   I CHOOSE TO (the old HAVE TO) because I get the reward/benefit of _____.

Give an example from your life. Give students 3-4 minutes.

8. Reinforce key points of what students can do (i.e., switch your attitude, focus on rewards/benefits, if you're going to do the task anyway choose the attitude you want, etc.).

IMPOSSIBLE? MAYBE NOT!

PURPOSE

1. To promote personal responsibility for one's actions.

2. To reinforce the power of the words one uses.

PROCEDURE

1. Have students partner up.

2. Have students make "I can't" statements back and forth with their partners (i.e., "I can't spell well," "I can't get a date.") Give them 2-3 minutes to brainstorm as many "I can't" statements as they can. Tell them to think of their lives at school, home, with friends and at work.

3. In the large group, have students share what that felt like to say the "I can'ts". Did they have reasons why they "can't" do something? Did these reasons start to come up when they were making the statements. Just accept their answers for now. This is more of an opportunity for them to become aware of their responses to the activity than to discuss them at length.

4. Still with their partners, ask students to repeat the same sentences changing the "I can't" to "I won't." They are not to change any other part of the statement (i.e., "I won't spell well," "I won't get a date.")

5. Again in the large group, discuss the feelings the students had doing this. Ask if there were any differences between saying "I can't," and "I won't." Once they had said the statement with "I won't," did "I can't" sound any different to them?

6. Have them think about whether their "I can't" statements were really impossible tasks or just ones they either refused to do, were scared or intimidated by, or didn't want to attempt. Have students think about their "I won't" statements. Were the "I won't" statements more honest than the "I can't" statements? Are there any "I can't" statements when stated that way, actually begin to look possible? Do any alternatives present themselves just by changing the wording.

DISCUSSION

Bring to the students' awareness that "I can't" implies being controlled from the outside, unable to do something, while "I won't" indicates a recognition of personal responsibility and being in charge of your own life. They have the right to refuse to do things (of course there are consequences for every action which they need to consider before refusing!) It is important that they acknowledge that right along with their power to choose to do something. The words they use to describe their lives and their attitudes have a strong impact upon their thinking and behavior. This last statement can generate a good debate.

NOTE: Begin to bring their "I can't" statements to the students' attention when they make them. Ask them to review if their "I can't" statements are, in fact, "I won't" statements.

CHANGING ATTITUDES

PURPOSE

1. To acknowledge attitudes that have been changed.

2. To explore attitudes to be changed.

3. To practice changing attitudes.

PROCEDURE

1. Review this information on attitudes with your students:

It is important that we examine our attitudes from time to time as our lives change and we find ourselves in new situations. Whether it's a new city, a new grade, a new job, or new friends, anytime things are "different", we're liable to discover some attitudes that may hold us back from achieving what we want. Some attitudes that used to work for us, may not anymore.

An example: There was a young man who hated anyone that didn't dress, eat, or act like he did. He had a negative attitude towards many people. His behavior wasn't very nice and people stayed away from him. The payoff he received was he got to stay angry (which he wanted to be), and he got to be "right" that all those other people didn't like him anyway. He was, however, very lonely.

He looked at his life and decided he wanted to have more friends. He began to like himself more and didn't want to be so angry. He began to change his attitude towards others. He found that other people just had different ways of dressing, talking, and acting, and that he didn't need to hate them so much. He found as his attitude became more positive, his behavior changed and people started to want to be with him more. He made friends, which made his attitude even more positive. He had been smart enough to change his attitude when he discovered the old one wasn't working anymore.

2. Review with students ways they have changed their attitudes about things in their lives.

For example, when they were little, they might have been frightened of water. Now, they may love water sports. The things that were causing them stress, the water, haven't changed. Their attitude has. If they're feeling stressed about something they can't change, they can perhaps change their attitude, and work with whatever it is, the best way they can.

3. Have students complete the activity sheet. Discuss ways students could change their attitudes to create the ones they want.

4. Play "Attitudes."

Students sit in a semi-circle. One student goes into the middle and pantomimes a negative attitude. Students call out guesses as to what the attitude is and what it is about (i.e., bored in class). The student that guesses comes into the middle and demonstrates a change in that attitude (i.e., finding interest in the activity in class). This doesn't need to be a pantomime. When the original student catches on, he/she shifts to the positive attitude. This game works best when it moves fast. It can be noisy, so be prepared.

OPTIONS

1. Play #4 as a drawing game. One student draws a person in a situation experiencing a negative attitude. The other students attempt to guess the attitude and the situation. The student that guesses correctly comes to the board and draws the positive shift in attitude. This can be done with teams in a game show style.

2. Have students get partners. In turn have each partner "Describe a time (or times) when you had every reason to have a negative attitude and you chose to have a positive one. (i.e., things went wrong and you laughed at yourself)."NOTE: Begin to bring their "I can't" statements to the students' attention when they make them. Ask them to review if their "I can't" statements are, in fact, "I won't" statements.

CHANGING ATTITUDES

ATTITUDES I'VE CHANGED

Step 1: Think about several events or situations that used to cause you stress, but because your attitude has changed, no longer upset you.
Step 2: Write the original feeling, reaction, or attitude you had to each situation.
Step 3: Write your present feeling, reaction, or attitude.

STEP 1: Event or Situation	STEP 2: Original Feeling (Reaction/Attitude)	STEP 3: Present Feeling (Reaction/Attitude)

ATTITUDES I'D LIKE TO CHANGE

Follow the same first 2 steps with several attitudes you have now that you'd like to change. These may be attitudes that are limiting you or are keeping you from achieving success. In step 3 write the feeling, reaction, or attitude you'd like to have towards this situation.

STEP 1: Event or Situation	STEP 2: Original Feeling (Reaction/Attitude)	STEP 3: Desired Feeling (Reaction/Attitude)

MAKING THE BEST OF ME

LEARNING FROM MISTAKES

PURPOSE

1. To neutralize the emotionally negative reaction to mistakes.

2. To recognize the importance of one's attitude that permits viewing mistakes as opportunities from which to learn.

PROCEDURE

Read and complete activity sheet.

DISCUSSION

1. Share mistakes and attitudes. Emphasize the importance of laughing at your own mistakes. Emphasize the difference between laughing at someone and with them.

2. Have students notice what kinds of mistakes affect them more negatively.

3. What buttons do those push?

4. Do you see any relationship between your attitudes and how you can use a mistake as an opportunity from which to learn and grow?

LEARNING FROM MISTAKES

Everybody makes mistakes. Mistakes are learning tools. They tell you what you need to learn. For instance, if you spell a word incorrectly on a spelling test, that tells you that you need to study that word some more. Thomas Edison made over 1,000 mistakes before he created the light bulb. Good thing he didn't quit! Quitting is what people sometimes choose to do after making a mistake.

What does a little baby do when it is first learning to walk? The baby falls . . . then what? The baby gets up and tries again. Have you ever heard a baby call out after falling, "Guess what, I am never going to try walking again in my life. I give up." Even if babies could talk, you wouldn't hear them say that. They just stand up one more time than they fall down. Soon they are learning how to walk.

When people make mistakes, they often say to themselves, "I'm not perfect so I must be bad." What if making mistakes means you're a human being? So a "mistake" is just an attempt that did not work. That's all.

In fact, mistakes can often lead to success through the adjustments you can make to correct them. Some mistakes are more useful than others. Your attitude about your mistakes has a lot to do with their effect on you. What if mistakes are leading you towards learning and success?

List 5 mistakes you have made:

1.
2.
3.
4.
5.

List what you could learn from each of these mistakes:

1.
2.
3.
4.
5.

MOCK ARGUMENT

PURPOSE

1. To build awareness of personal observation skills.

2. To experience the nature of how points of views are developed.

3. To notice how assumptions can be made against oneself or others.

PROCEDURE

1. Decide upon a "mock" argument between you and a student. Possible scenarios are:

   Student comes by your desk and, in a way obvious to the class, tosses a note on your desk (or at you). You read it and feign being angry and demand that the student leave the class (i.e., go to the counselor's office, etc.). The student storms out, but actually just waits outside the door.

   Student comes into class late.

   Student is whispering or calling out.

   (In each situation the teacher and student would have a confrontation resulting in the student leaving the room.)

2. Choose a student ahead of time who will be your "accomplice," and review and practice the mock argument with him.

3. After the argument occurs and the student leaves the room, there is often a moment of surprise. Still "in character", you can begin a discussion with the class.

   "What actually happened here?" (Get more points of view. Allow students to recount what they each actually saw and heard as well as their opinions of who was in the "right" and who was in the "wrong.")

4. Then have your "accomplice" come back in the room and tell the whole story (i.e., that he and you planned the scene.)

5. Go right into further discussion.

DISCUSSION

1. What was this all about?

2. Were there various points of view in the class of what "actually" happened? If so, why?

3. Were there various points of view in the class on who was "right"? Why?

4. Share experiences where you jumped to a conclusion and made assumptions against others that were inaccurate.

5. Share experiences where people "did something" to you that you assumed was against you but really wasn't.

6. Do you have any feelings about my "setting you up?" Was the activity valuable?

7. What did you learn about yourself or others?

OPTIONS

1. At the point that the accomplice has left the room, students can be asked to write their observations on a sheet of paper and then have them read aloud. This allows for everyone noting their personal observation without any external influence.

2. The discussion questions can be used as a written assignment on observation skills, assumptions, or points of view.

ARE YOUR FEELINGS DRIVING YOU?

PURPOSE

To explore the degree to which we allow our feelings to control us.

PROCEDURE

Each student fills out an activity sheet.

OPTIONS

1. Explore, as a group, the questions at the bottom of the activity sheet.

2. Brainstorm ways to become more in charge of your feelings.

3. Is there a difference between ignoring a feeling and not letting it "drive" you?

4. What are the advantages of each method?

5. Does not letting your feelings drive you make you boring?

6. Are there times when it is better not to act on a feeling you have? When? How is it better?

ARE YOUR FEELINGS DRIVING YOU?

Describe an event or a situation in your life in which you felt each of the feelings listed below.

Example: I felt MOTIVATED to do my best when I saw my girlfriend watching me.

1. I felt **proud**

2. I felt **disappointed**

3. I felt **responsible**

4. I felt **anxious**

5. I felt **surprised**

6. I felt **sympathetic**

7. I felt **exhausted**

8. I felt **befriended**

9. I felt **lonely**

10. I felt **angry**

11. I felt **embarrassed**

12. I felt **discouraged**

13. I felt **mature**

14. I felt **excited**

List some different ways your feelings affected your behavior:

Would you have acted differently if you had had a different feeling?

Who is in charge of your feelings?

LETTING GO OF JUDGMENT AND GUILT

PURPOSE

1. To gain an understanding of the role judgment and guilt play in our lives.

2. To practice tools for letting go of stored judgment and guilt.

PROCEDURE

1. Discuss judgment and guilt with students.

Guilt is anger directed against ourselves. It occurs when you get angry with yourself for something you tell yourself you should have done or shouldn't have done. Guilt can create tremendous feelings of unworthiness and self-hatred.

Some of the keys for letting go of guilt are:

    1. Know that no one is perfect.

    2. Realize that we all make mistakes and can consciously learn from them.

    3. Be wise and accept your shortcomings.

    4. Forgive yourself.

    5. Rather than mulling over the past, move on to what's next. If possible, take corrective action.

2. Review the activity sheet questions with the students.

3. Have the students choose partners and complete the activity.

DISCUSSION

1. What are some of the "shoulds" that you've been placing on yourself?

2. What were some of the ways you discovered you could let go of self-judgments?

3. If you judge other people a lot, might it be an indication that you inwardly judge yourself?

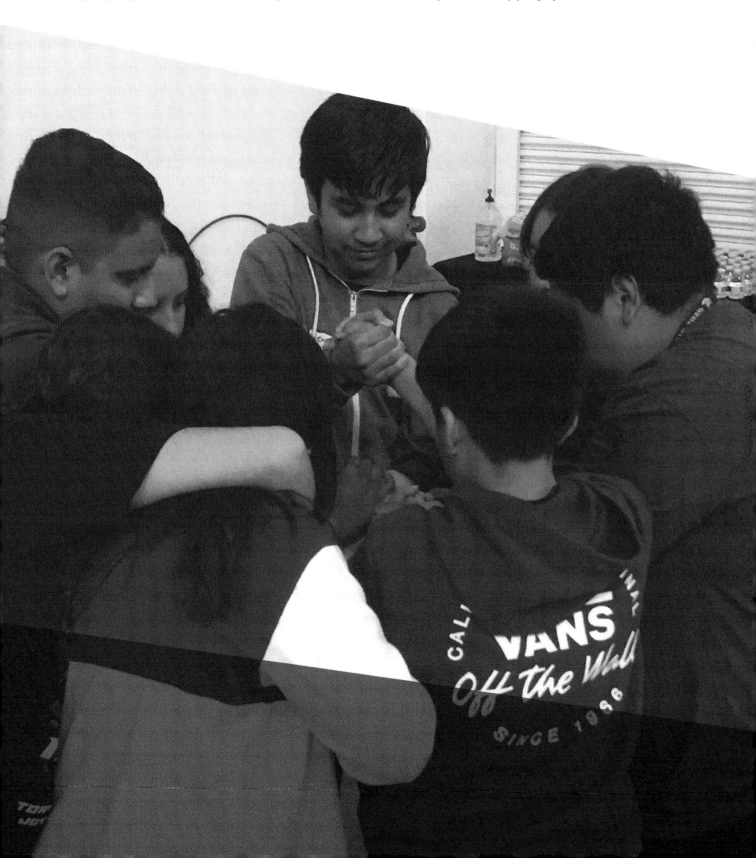

LETTING GO OF JUDGMENT AND GUILT

The following series of questions can be done individually as a written activity or verbally, with a partner. Cycle through the questions, answering them several times before switching partners. Finish each set of answers by writing/stating the last sentence.

For example:

1. What do you judge about yourself?

    I judge my intelligence. I think others are smarter than I am. Others get better grades than I do, so I must be stupid.

2. What do you believe "should" be different about yourself?

    I "should" be smarter and be getting better grades.

3. Is there anything you can do about that?

    I can spend more time studying. I can ask for assistance. I can talk to others and find out how they are getting good grades.

4. How can you let go of the judgment inside yourself?

    I can forgive myself. I can realize that I have done what I have done up until now and acknowledge that I've done the best I knew how at the time. I can accept my best effort and forgive myself for judging myself.

5. How can you be more caring for yourself?

    I can accept myself the way I am. I can acknowledge myself for ways that I am already expressing my intelligence. I can practice and develop my intelligence more. I can reward myself when I get better grades.

6. Will you do that? (Be honest here!)

    Yes!

"I AM ACCEPTING AND LOVING MYSELF."

1. What do you judge about yourself?

2. What do you believe "should" be different about yourself?

3. Is there anything you can do about that?

4. How can you let go of the judgment inside yourself?

5. How can you be more caring for yourself?

6. Will you do that?

"I AM ACCEPTING AND LOVING MYSELF."

LETTING GO OF RESENTMENT

PURPOSE

1. To gain an understanding of the role resentment plays in life.

2. To learn and practice keys to letting go of stored resentments.

PROCEDURE

1. Discuss resentment with students.

Resentment is anger directed at others. You get angry with others for something you tell yourself they should or shouldn't have done. With resentment, you often avoid or isolate yourself from others. It destroys relationships and limits your growth and understanding. It hurts and can even create disease and illness. You don't have to live in resentment. Often, you will pay the price for resentment more than the person you feel justified in resenting.

2. Review some of the keys for letting go of resentment.

    1. Realize that you don't have to hold on to having to be "right" and making someone else "wrong," either in their opinions, expressions or actions.

    2. Knowing that just as you can accept yourself as not always being "perfect," so can you allow others to be "human" and to make mistakes.

    3. Forgive them.

    4. Communicate honesty and caring directly to the people involved.

    5. Put yourself in their shoes. Perhaps they have had a difficult day, a troubled past, etc.

    6. Realize that blame can be a "cop-out" for not being willing to take responsibility for what you can do to make the situation and your life better.

3. The activity questions can be done individually, as a written activity or verbally with a partner. Explain to the students how you want them to complete the activity.

DISCUSSION

1. People have "excellent" reasons to hold on to resentment. However, who really suffers from resentment?

2. Can you change people's behavior?

3. Do you like it when people try to change your behavior?

4. How can you learn to be more accepting of yourself and others?

LETTING GO OF RESENTMENT

The following series of questions can be done individually as a written activity or verbally, with a partner. Cycle through the questions, answering them several times before switching partners. Finish each set of answers by writing/stating the last sentence.

For example:

1. What do you judge about others?

    I judge my sister for saying mean things to me.

2. What do you believe "should" be different about them?

    She should be kinder to me and treat me with greater respect.

3. Is there anything you can do about that?

    I can either accept her behavior and care for her anyway or I can let her know that I don't like how she speaks to me and I'd like her to treat me better.

4. How can you let go of the judgment inside of yourself?

    I realize that she is having a hard time herself with things in her life. I can forgive her and know that she's not always the perfect sister (and I'm not the perfect sister/brother either.)

5. How can you be more caring?

    I can be open to telling her the ways I do appreciate her and care for her, even if she's not "perfect". I can also do what I can to assist her and be honest with her.

6. Will you do that? (Be honest here!)

    Yes!

"MY CARING FOR MYSELF AND FOR _____ IS MORE IMPORTANT
(fill in their name)
THAN MY RESENTMENT. I AM ACCEPTING THEM AS THEY ARE."

1. What do you judge about others?

2. What do you believe "should" be different about them?

3. Is there anything you can do about that?

4. How can you let go of the judgment inside of yourself?

5. How can you be more caring?

6. Will you do that? (Be honest here!)

"MY CARING FOR MYSELF AND FOR _____ IS MORE IMPORTANT
(fill in their name)
THAN MY RESENTMENT. I AM ACCEPTING THEM AS THEY ARE."

RISK EXERCISE

PURPOSE

1. To heighten awareness of risk taking behavior.

2. To examine motivating factors in risking or not risking.

PROCEDURE

1. Ask for five volunteers to come up in front of the group to do "something." Do not tell the class what it is or give them anymore information.

2. Once the volunteers have come up front, tell them that they have just completed the "something." Ask each to share with the class why they came up front and how they felt.

3. Have the class give them applause once they've finished talking.

DISCUSSION

1. Why did you not choose to come up front? (Be careful to not make them wrong for not volunteering.)

2. What were you afraid of? Is that fear real or imagined?

3. What's the difference between "imagined" fear (little or no reality base) and "real" fear (reality based)? (i.e., Imagined fear: "When I grow up I may die with no friends." Reality-based fear: "There are bees swarming towards me right now. Move.")

4. Describe times in your life when you let "imagined" fear block you from getting involved. (i.e., calling a new girl or boyfriend on the phone, telling someone your honest feelings, etc.)

5. Can risk-taking ever be reckless and harmful? What's the difference between risking recklessly versus risking wisely?

6. What's the benefit in risking wisely?

7. What "wise" risks might you want to do more of in your life? at school? with you family? with your friends? with yourself?

OPTIONS

Have students decide on one wise risk they are willing to take this week. Have them report back on it the next week.

I SCARE MYSELF

PURPOSE

1. To promote responsibility for the emotion of fear.

2. To practice taking charge of fear.

PART A

PROCEDURE

1. Write the word FEAR on the board. Ask students to call out what they are afraid of and write these around the word.

2. Have students find a partner. Give the students 2-3 minutes to complete this sentence, back and forth.

"I am afraid to: _____."

3. Then give the students another 2-3 minutes to use the same fears and change each statement to:

"I'd really like to _____."

"And I scare myself by imagining _____."

DISCUSSION

1. Did the experience of the fear change as you changed the wording? How?

2. Can you see how you sometimes stop yourself from doing things you want to do by creating fear?

3. Have you ever done something even though you were afraid? Did your imagined expectations occur?

PART B

PROCEDURE

1. Write FEAR vertically to create an acronym:

   F antasized
   E xpectations
   A ppearing
   R eal

2. Discuss the acronym.

3. Reform partnerships and have them cycle through the following questions, using an example from the students' list to demonstrate.

   Example:

   A. What are you afraid of?

   I'm afraid of losing my best friend.

   B. Has it happened yet?

   No.

   C. Is it happening now?

   No.

   D. Might it happen in the future?

   Yes

   E. Are you acting as though the "future maybe" (or expectation) is real now?

   Yes.

   F. What could you do to be more present now?

   Focus on the relationship I have with him/her now.

You may want to post the questions for easy reference.

DISCUSSION

1. Do you feel like you have more control over your fear?

2. How did you get it?

3. What did you discover about yourself?

MEET THE PRESS

PURPOSE

1. To experience taking moderate risks in a supportive environment.

2. To demonstrate support and respect for classmates.

3. To enhance communication skills.

PROCEDURE

1. Ask for a volunteer to do a mystery activity. Use a lottery system if there is more than one volunteer.

2. The volunteer sits in front of the room. Announce that this is to be a press conference in which the remaining students will interview the volunteer. The students may ask any question they wish, but the volunteer has the right to say "no comment" on any question he/she does not choose to answer.

3. At the end of 5 minutes, break in, thank the volunteer and end the press conference. The volunteer may wish to end the press conference before that time. To do so, he/she may simply say "Thank you very much," and return to his/her seat.

Suggestion: As the teacher, take a turn, as well. Your willingness to risk can assist the students in their risk-taking.

4. Repeat as many times as you choose.

DISCUSSION

1. Did you feel supported by the group while being interviewed? How?

2. What was it like to volunteer? To not volunteer?

3. Was it risky to be the volunteer? If so, was it worth taking the risk?

TAKE A STAND

PURPOSE

1. To heighten awareness of the personal characteristics and preferences of all members of the class.

2. To point out those things that they have in common.

PROCEDURE

1. An issue or question is presented to the class and written on the board.

2. Draw a line on the board and divide it into five segments and number each segment one through five. The end points represent opposite positions of a continuum.

3. Ask students to suggest phrases that define the two extremes. (For examples, see the following page.) The middle three positions are kept constant or filled in by the teacher to keep the activity moving.

4. Designate specific areas in the room where everyone who chooses the same number can stand together.

5. Students write the numbers 1 through 5 on 3" x 5" cards, one number to a card.

6. As each question or issue is presented, each student and the teacher selects the number that best represents his/her view without showing anyone else.

7. When all have selected their number on a particular question, then everyone moves to the designated area in the room for that specific number.

DISCUSSION

1. Were you surprised to see anyone with you in your group? Who? Why?

2. Were you surprised to see anyone in a different group?

3. Has anyone been in your group for all questions so far? Who?

4. Was there anyone you expected to be in your group who was not?

5. Was anyone tempted to change their mind based upon what someone else chose? Discuss how we can be influenced by others.

OPTIONS

1. For a quicker version, just have students raise their hands for the point in the continuum which relates to them.

2. Have students generate the issues presented.

3. For each continuum, students can share their reasons for placing themselves where they have.

Sample questions for "Take A Stand?" lesson

1. How much do you talk on the phone?

Never — All the time

2. How neat is your locker?

Messy — So So — Neat

3. How late do you sleep on Sunday mornings?

Up at dawn — Sleep until noon

4. How well do you like math? (Repeat for other curriculum areas)

Hate it — Love it

5. How well do you confront others about a problem?

Very Awkward — Easily

6. Are you more of a morning person or a night person?

Morning — Night

7. How much of a listener are you?

Rarely listen — Listen a lot

8. How fair do you think your teacher is?

Not fair — Fair

9. How much time do you spend studying each day?

None — Five Hours

10. How many times a day would you prefer to eat?

1 — 10

I AGREE/I DISAGREE

PURPOSE

1. To encourage active and spontaneous decision-making.

2. To accept individual differences.

PROCEDURE

1. Have all students seated in circle.

2. Demonstrate five different ways people can vote or express their opinions on an issue. If you . . .

> *Strongly agree: wave both hands in air, shout, cheer, etc.*
> *Agree: put your thumb up*
> *Strongly disagree: shake head "no" while calling out "no"*
> *Disagree: put your thumb down*
> *No opinion: fold arms across chest*

3. Then in quick sequence, make controversial statements appropriate to age level and interests of the group.

Examples might be:

> *"Students should be paid to attend school."*
> *"I would discourage my son/daughter from premarital sex."*
> *"Cheating on tests is sometimes okay."*
> *"If your best friend is taking drugs, it's best*
>   *. . . to tell his mother/father about it."*
>   *. . . to talk to him about what you think."*
>   *. . . to do nothing about it."*
> *"The cashier at the department store gives you back an extra $5 in change. It's best to keep the cash and say nothing about it."*

4. Come up with or have the class come up with their own value statements/questions.

DISCUSSION

1. How is this type of voting different from other voting you've done?

2. Did your friends vote the same way you did? Does this matter?

3. Did you change your vote after you looked around you?

4. Were you concerned about what others thought of you and your opinions?

5. What did you learn about yourself/the group?

CAN I QUOTE YOU ON THAT?

PURPOSE

1. To enhance awareness of personal values.

2. Increase group cohesiveness.

PROCEDURE

1. Choose a quotation by a famous person about some topic and write it on the blackboard. You might want to have a book or two of quotes available for easy reference for you and the students.

2. Lead a discussion about what the quote means to each person.

3. Ask students to write a statement which reflects their ideas and values on the subject.

   Example Quotes:

   "Trust men and they will be true to you; treat them greatly and they will show themselves great."
   - Ralph Waldo Emerson

   "Life consists not in holding the good cards but playing those you do hold well." - Josh Billings

   "To get rid of an enemy, one must love him." - Leo Tolstoy

   "Don't let life discourage you; everyone who got where he is had to begin where he was."
   - Richard L. Evans

   "Nonviolence is a weapon of the strong." - Mahatma Gandhi

OPTIONS

1. Form small groups. Have the groups come up with their own quote and expand on it.

2. Take time to discuss their quotes.

3. Produce a booklet of class quotes separated by subject. (i.e., friendship, honesty, risking, etc.)

4. Create a collage of pictures from magazines, newspapers, and personal drawings that expresses the meaning of a chosen quotation.

5. Create a bulletin board that students can fill with 3x5 index cards with favorite quotations decorated as they choose.

6. Create a page of favorite quotes that students can keep in their personal journals.

VIEWPOINTS IN THE ROUND

PURPOSE

1. To provide structure for students to express their views.

2. To encourage the learning of relevant topics.

3. To practice seeing issues from different points of view.

PROCEDURE

1. Arrange 6 chairs in a circle at the front of the room.

2. Ask for 5 volunteers to sit in the circle to express their views on a given topic. The extra chair is saved for anyone in the class who wants to come in and briefly add some information to the debate (facts, dates, etc.), after which, the student returns to his/her seat.

3. Students in the circle are to be silent until each viewpoint has been heard.

4. After each person in the circle has expressed his/her point of view and the group has discussed the topic, invite other students to ask questions of the group members and to give their own points of view.

   Suggested topics:

   1. Are nuclear weapons a good idea for this country to develop?
   2. How can people resist peer pressure to use cigarettes, alcohol or drugs?
   3. Is it important to go to college?
   4. Should there be a dress code at school?

5. A new group can be formed with a new topic or the activity can be repeated another day.

DISCUSSION

1. Did you change your viewpoint after hearing others' comments?

2. Did you understand others' point of view more than you did before?

3. Did this affect your attitude in any way?

4. Did you feel people were listening attentively to each other?

5. How did you feel being inside the circle?

6. How did you feel being outside the circle?

7. Did you feel listened to? Is this a new feeling for you?

BROKEN AGREEMENTS

PURPOSE

1. To examine the impact of broken agreements on trust and relationships.

2. To learn and practice keys for keeping agreements.

PROCEDURE

1. Discuss the results of making and breaking agreements in life.

An agreement is like a "promise" we make with ourselves or someone else.

Sometimes we make agreements with other people, and, when we do so, we nonetheless make the same agreement with ourselves. It is very important that we keep our agreements.

Every time we say we will do something, there is a part of us that listens to what we say. This part of us listens to and records every agreement we make.

If we act differently than what we have said, then we have broken our agreement with ourself. When we do, we automatically pay the following prices:

1. Loss of trust from others

2. Relationships weakened

3. Loss of self-trust, self-esteem, self-respect, self-approval and self-worth

4. More self-doubt

5. Lack of clarity

6. Tiredness and confusion

When we make promises to ourselves like, "I'm definitely getting up at 6 am tomorrow," or, "I'm doing my homework tonight," and then not do what we said we would, we pay these automatic prices. Whether we break our word by a "little" (getting up at 6:15) or by a lot (getting up at noon), we still pay a price. There is a part of us within us who listens to our agreements, big or small.

If we keep the agreements (promises) we make, then we begin to "believe" that we can do what we say, and we "automatically" receive the following rewards:

1. Greater trust by others

2. Relationships improved

3. Greater self-trust, self-esteem, self-respect, self-approval and self-worth

4. Greater self-confidence

5. Greater clarity

6. More energy, more vitality

2. Present and discuss these four tips for keeping agreements (promises):

1. MAKE AGREEMENTS IMPORTANT

Whether you think your agreement is important (getting to a concert on time) or unimportant, (helping your younger brother clean the garage) if you agreed to it, make it important to complete. If you make the agreement important to you, it will be easier for you to keep it.

2. WRITE YOUR AGREEMENTS DOWN

Make a list of your agreements (see "Daily Goals" and "Weekly Planner", Chapter 5) so that you can easily remember. You can put these on a calendar and review it each day. Check them off when you do them.

3. MAKE FEWER AGREEMENTS

Have you ever told several people you would do something for the same night or weekend and found yourself "swamped?" This is called overcommitting. Practice making fewer promises and keep the ones that you make. Sometimes it means telling people, "No, I'd like to but I have other plans."

4. COMMUNICATE IF YOU NEED TO MAKE A CHANGE IN YOUR AGREEMENT

For instance, if you realize that you started late and won't be at your friend's house on time, it pays to call and let him/her know.

BROKEN AGREEMENTS

Recall times at home, at school, or elsewhere, with yourself or with others, recently or in the past, where you gave your word and then did not keep it. Fill in the chart below with some examples from your life.

TIMES I BROKE MY AGREEMENTS (with myself or others)	"PRICE" I PAID
For example: Last Saturday I told my dad I'd clean my room and I didn't	Dad got angry with me and doesn't trust I'll do what I say I'm going to do.
1.	1.
2.	2.
3.	3.
4.	4.
5.	5.

Recall times at home, at school or elsewhere, with yourself or with others, recently or in the past, where you gave your word and then kept it. Fill in the chart below with examples from your life.

TIMES I KEPT MY AGREEMENTS (with myself or others)	"REWARDS" I RECEIVED
For example: *Last night I decided to get to bed by 10 pm and I did.*	*I feel more energetic and awake today. I trust myself more.*
1.	1.
2.	2.
3.	3.
4.	4.
5.	5.

What I have learned about keeping my agreements is:

What I will do better in order to keep my agreements is:

TAKING CHARGE

PURPOSE

1. To enhance awareness of the degree to which students take personal responsibility for their actions.

2. To identify areas in which students wish to take greater responsibility.

3. To enhance group cohesiveness.

PROCEDURE

1. Have students fill out activity sheet.

2. After the students identify areas for desired improvement, ask them to write three or more ways they can begin to take charge of these areas of their lives.

3. Now have them write three negative habits or attitudes they'll give up by taking charge (i.e., being able to blame others, avoiding responsibilities.) Have them be specific.

4. Finally have them write three things or benefits they'll be gaining by taking charge (i.e., gaining more self-confidence.)

5. Determine check-in or review times to assess progress. This can be done as a group or in partners.

DISCUSSION

Write responses to #3 and #4 above on the board and discuss.

TAKING CHARGE

How would you rate yourself in each of these situations below? In the rating column, write a number from 1 to 4 to indicate the degree to which you feel you are in charge of your behavior.

1 - I tend to be out of control in this situation.
2 - I tend to depend on adults for direction in this situation.
3 - I tend to be in charge of myself some of the time in this situation.
4 - I tend to be in charge of myself most of the time in this situation.

RATING   **SITUATION**

_____ 1. Getting myself up in the morning

_____ 2. Getting to school on time

_____ 3. Completing class assignments

_____ 4. Completing homework assignments

_____ 5. Studying for tests

_____ 6. Using my class time wisely

_____ 7. Making new friends

_____ 8. Working with a partner

_____ 9. Cleaning up my room

_____ 10. Organizing my time

_____ 11. Keeping track of my assignments

_____ 12. Doing my chores at home

_____ 13. Keeping my curfew

_____ 14. Limiting the amount of TV I watch

_____ 15. Trying new activities

What overall rating (1, 2, 3, or 4) describes you best?

Place a star (*) in front of the two areas you would most like to improve.

CHAPTER 5
Achieving Excellence

TEACHING TIPS & SUGGESTIONS

This chapter builds and expands upon the foundation work established in the previous chapter. As students develop the concept of personal responsibility, they are then more ready to step forward and learn the practical skills that produce results.

1 It is suggested that the activities on goal setting be introduced after a thorough exploration of the earlier activities in the chapter. As students develop their own dreams and clear intentions of what they want, the goal setting work has more meaning and substance. The order of the activities in this chapter is important to follow. The fundamental skills for goal setting are introduced step by step to allow for the most effective use. Use them in a consolidated way. You may want to introduce this chapter as a month long "Achieving Excellence" unit.

2 Many teenagers literally live outside their own control. They feel as if they are being controlled by other forces. They unconsciously ask for skills to gain personal control over their lives. Two very effective ways for students to experience control of their own lives are for them to learn to:

- set goals and achieve them

- make commitments or promises and then keep them

Goal setting skills can provide students with a sense of confidence in knowing they can effectively achieve their desired results.

3 Stay close at hand as your students work with their goals. Setting goals may be very new for many students. Often, they will approach personal goals and objectives with a history of failure, guilt, disappointment, or fear of disapproval from others. Past negative beliefs may limit them at the outset. Your encouragement and clarity in working individually with them is needed.

4 Goal setting is not meant to be a guilt-producer. It can be used as an incredible framework for building "the winning habit." Have your students start off with goals that are simple and achievable. Then over time as they develop and recognize that they are winning on their goals, they can stretch more and choose more challenging goals.

5 Practice the goal setting skills yourself. Doing them along with your students can be a powerful asset in understanding their process.

ACTIVITY PREVIEWS

GETTING WHAT YOU WANT
Focus: Group game bringing awareness to getting what you want in life.
Time: 20 min.

A NEW REALITY
Focus: Develop future vision in preparation for goal-setting.
Time: 20 minutes
Activity: Page V-08

WHY GO TO SCHOOL ANYWAY?
Focus: Written activity to examine role of school in achieving success.
Time: 15 minutes
Activity: Page V-12

DREAMING
Focus: Create dream/vision to prepare for a future goal-setting.
Time: 20 minutes
Activity: Page V-16

KING/QUEEN OF THE WORLD
Focus: Expand out of conventional thinking in preparation for goal-setting.
Time: 20-30 minutes

CREATING THE NEW YEAR
Focus: Plan and visualize a successful new year; interactive or written activity.
Time: Varies - 30 minutes
Activity: Page V-21

THE SUCCESSES OF MY LIFE
Focus: Acknowledgment and projection of past and future successes.
Time: 30 minutes
Activity: Page V-27

FROM LIMITATION INTO EXPANSION
Focus: Explore, identify, and shift limiting beliefs.
Time: 2 class sessions
Activity: Page V-31

THE DATA DUMP
Focus: Compile list of incompletions and set strategy to complete tasks.
Time: Varies - can be done outside of class

CYCLE OF ACTION
Focus: Triad activity bringing awareness to habits of task completion.
Time: 40-50 minutes
Activity: Page V-37

MAGNIFICENCE
Focus: Acknowledge our specialness and the qualities necessary to create success in our lives.
Time: 50 minutes

CREATIVE VISUALIZATIONS
Focus: An individual activity with teacher introduction on the value and use of creative visualizations; a preparation for goal setting.
Time: 30 minutes
Activity: Page V-42

IDEAL SCENE
Focus: Establish ideal scene for life in preparation for goal-setting.
Time: 10-20 minutes
Activity: Page V-45

MIND MAPPING
Focus: A hands-on activity to spark creativity and problem-solving; a preparation for goal setting.
Time: 30 minutes
Activity: Page V-47

GOAL SETTING - PART 1 (GUIDELINES)
Focus: Introduction to the general principles for effective goal setting.
Time: 30 minutes
Activity: Page V-50

GOAL SETTING - PART 2 (ACTION PLAN)
Focus: An activity to clarify specific action steps for completing a project/goal.
Time: 30 minutes
Activity: Page V-54

DAILY GOALS
Focus: A weekly chart to evaluate progress on self-directed daily goals.
Time: 5-10 minutes each day for one week.
Activity: Page V-57

WEEKLY PLANNER
Focus: A calendar for weekly school and personal activities.
Time: 15 minutes first time; then 3-5 minutes daily at home or at school.
Activity: Page V-60

SIX STEPS TO ACHIEVING EXCELLENCE
Focus: A review of the techniques for goal setting by taking on one goal and developing it through all six steps to completion.
Time: Varies (extended activity over several days or weeks)
Activity: Page V-64

MANAGING MONEY
Focus: Examine attitudes regarding money.
Time: 30-40 minutes
Activity: Page V-68

TREASURE MAPS
Focus: A personal collage project where students create a physical representation of what they want.
Time: 2-3 hours

THE WEEK IN REVIEW - 1
Focus: Become aware of the week's progress and provide direction for growth.
Time: 10-20 minutes
Activity: Page V-74

THE WEEK IN REVIEW - 2
Focus: Build group trust through sharing about the week's occurrences.
Time: 10-15 minutes

GETTING WHAT YOU WANT

PURPOSE

1. To identify the frequency each student gets what he/she wants in life.

2. To generate ideas as to how to get more of what they really want.

3. To enhance group cohesiveness.

PROCEDURE

1. Put up a large sign on one end of the room that says, "I Never Get What I Really Want," and one at the other end saying, "I Always Get What I Really Want."

2. Lay out two or three strings on the floor about two feet apart reaching from one sign to the other.

3. Ask the students to place themselves along the line at the point that indicates how they experience their own lives in terms of their ability to create what they want. Suggest that "honesty" is the key in this exercise. "This is to be done in silence. At some point there may be many of you at the same place on the string, just line up side by side between the strings that are laid out on the floor."

4. After the line has formed, ask the students to form a group of four from those closest to them along the string. Each person will then have 1-3 minutes to share about the reasons for their position and their feelings about the point they have chosen on the string.

Example: "Well, I'm not too happy because it seems I hardly ever get what I want, and I really don't know why." or "I seem to be an instantaneous success at almost everything I do. I was surprised by how few of us chose this point along the line."

5. Ask students to brainstorm why they may be at the point along the line that they are. Do they communicate what they want? Do they say its okay when they don't get it? Do they demand it? How valid are their wants in terms of their own well being (i.e., drugs, alcohol, etc. may not serve them)?

6. Ask students at the "Never" end of the scale to share the beliefs they have about getting what they want (i.e., "It takes hard work," or "I'm not lucky."). List these on the board.

7. Now ask students closer to the "Always" end of the scale to share their beliefs about getting what they want. ("I enjoy asking for what I want." "I'm good at getting what I want.") List these on the board.

DISCUSSION

1. Note the differences between the lists. Discuss these.

2. How do your beliefs affect whether you get what you want in life?

3. What did you learn about why you are at the point on the scale you are on? How might you improve your position?

OPTIONS

Repeat this activity after a month and note changes with the students.

A NEW REALITY

PURPOSE

1. To increase awareness of future vision for self.

2. To enhance group trust through sharing.

3. To set foundation for creation of goals.

PROCEDURE

1. Students complete activity sheet.

2. Writing on the back of the sheet or recording their comments, students turn the answers into present tense reality. Instead of futurizing, students mock-up being the person they want to be. They can write their pieces as TV News spots, informational newspaper columns, book jackets, etc. They can use whatever supplies they need to express the idea.

3. Students share their new realities with the group.

OPTIONS

Students have a "mixer" type party, playing the part of their new reality roles. As they talk with one another they relate the answers to the activity sheet questions as present tense occurrences and skills in their lives.

DISCUSSION

1. How does it feel to be who you want to be?

2. Were you happy with what you created?

3. What do you need to do to create that new reality in your life?

4. Discuss any fears, limiting beliefs, etc., that came up during the activity.

A NEW REALITY

Complete the sentences below.

1. I want to become:

2. After I finish school I would like to:

3. As an adult, I think I would enjoy:

4. If I were to change one thing about me, I'd change:

because:

5. I'd like to be more:

and less:

6. If I could live anyplace in the world, I'd live:

7. To do what I'd like to do as an adult, I will probably need to learn about:

8. I will need to develop the following skills:

1.

2.

3.

4.

9. Three words that would describe my life as an adult would be:

1.

2.

3.

10. Three words to describe how I'd like my life to be in 3 months are:

1.

2.

3.

WHY GO TO SCHOOL ANYWAY?

PURPOSE

1. To clarify individual needs and expectations of school experience.

2. To increase awareness of value of school in achieving goals.

PROCEDURE

Complete the activity sheet.

DISCUSSION

1. What did you learn from this activity?

2. How do you feel about question number seven?

3. How many of you have asked for what you need?

4. How many are willing to?

5. How can this activity affect your motivation in school?

6. How is school valuable if you don't know your future career goals?

WHY GO TO SCHOOL ANYWAY?

Do you ever think about why you are in school and what you expect to get out of it? The questions below are designed to help clarify things for you.

1. What specific skills do you think you will learn in school this year?

2. What specific skills would you like to be learning this year in school?

3. For what occupation are you directing yourself?

4. What skills do you think you'll need to be successful in that job?

5. Which of these skills can school assist you in learning?

    In what way?

6. What skills could you be working on this year?

7. What do you think your teacher could do to assist you in developing these skills more fully?

Which teacher?

Have you asked him/her for this assistance?

If not, will you?

Explain:

DREAMING

PURPOSE

1. To create a dream or vision.

2. To explore wishes and desires.

3. To create a framework for goal setting.

PROCEDURE

Complete the activity sheet.

DISCUSSION

Share answers and allow the group to dream, expanding and elaborating on their visions. You might want to leave the students with the unanswered thought - "Are these dreams impossible or might they be possible to create into reality?"

DREAMING

Answer the questions below. Allow yourself to dream without limitation.

1. What type of car would you like to own?

Why?

2. If you could invent something, what would it be, what would it do?

Why would you want to invent it?

3. If you could be a famous person, who would you like to be?

Why?

4. In which period of time, past or future, would you like to live?

Why?

5. What skill or ability would you most like to possess?

Why?

6. Where in the United States would you like to visit?

Why?

7. What foreign country would you most like to visit?

Why?

8. Where in the world would you most like to live?

Why?

9. In which activity (sport, dance, etc.) would you like to be a star?

Why?

10. If you had a million dollars, what would you do with it?

11. What one change would you make if you were to become Leader of the World?

KING/QUEEN OF THE WORLD

PURPOSE

1. Encourage students to expand "possibility" thinking.

2. Prepare for goal setting activities.

PROCEDURE

1. Have students imagine themselves as the King or Queen of the whole world for one day. Limitless possibilities exist. Students can fantasize whatever they want. The only limit is the one day time limit. Ask the students to dream of all of the incredible opportunities that could exist for them and others in the world if they used that day to the fullest.

2. Have them write and share their visions and dreams of what they would do with that day, knowing that how they use their power and authority during the course of that day could affect not only their lives but the lives of everyone. Describe the day in as much detail as possible.

DISCUSSION

1. Are you surprised by the similarities or differences in each person's day?

2. What if each of us has more personal power than we assume? How can you use your personal power to create more of what you want for yourself and for others?

3. What does your special day tell you about what you consider important in your life?

OPTIONS

Students can write or share "I learned" statements based on what they have learned about themselves through doing this activity.

CREATING THE NEW YEAR

PURPOSE

1. To create a vision or plan for a successful new year.

2. To reflect on the learnings of the past year and use them as stepping stones into the next.

PROCEDURE

1. Students can answer the questions on the activity sheet in cooperation with a partner or a small group of friends. In either case, the most effective process seems to be one in which they answer one question, the next person answers the same question, and so on. No one in the group may go to the next question until the entire group has completed each question. If you choose to have students do this alone, have them write their answers out and take their time. You might choose to have them do just a few questions each day.

2. Students complete activity sheet.

OPTIONS

1. Discuss student's plans in a large group, small groups, or partners.

2. Create a bulletin board to display student plans. Students may want to add pictures, quotes, etc.

CREATING THE NEW YEAR

You will be learning some new things about yourself as you review last year. Enjoy your experience of creating a fantastic new year!

1. What was your biggest triumph in this past year?

2. What do you imagine your biggest triumph of next year will be?

3. List three very special times you had during the past year. *Circle the one that you most enjoyed.*
   1.
   2.
   3.

4. List three disappointments you had during the past year.
   1.
   2.
   3.

5. What are you going to do in the new year to avoid repeating those disappointments?

6. What was something that turned out better than expected in the past year?

7. Other than yourself, who was the most important person in your life in the past year?

8. Who do you think will be the most important person in your life next year?

Why?

9. What is the one thing you are most committed to doing in the new year?

10. If you accomplish this, how will it change your life? What would you like to be able to say about it one year from today?

11. What was the biggest decision you made in the past year, and how did it turn out?

12. What decision did you make in the past year that you wish you hadn't?

13. What decision didn't you make in the past year that you wish you had made?

14. What are you willing to do to make better decisions in the new year?

15. What is the biggest decision you think you will have to make in the new year?

16. Are you more or less optimistic about your chances for greater success than you were at the beginning of the past year?

17. What do you feel makes you a better, more deserving person today than you were a year ago?

18. What is the favorite object you bought in the past year?

19. What is the most rewarding compliment you received in the past year?

20. What is one compliment you wanted to give to another in the past year and didn't?

21. Who is someone you just met in the past year and would like to get to know better in the new year?

22. What is the biggest risk you took in the past year?

23. What do you think your biggest risk may be in the new year?

24. What in the past year totally surprised you?

25. If you could have three wishes granted for the new year, what would they be?
1.
2.
3.

26. What one word sums up the entire past year for you?

27. What is the most useful thing you learned in the past year?

28. What specific thing would you like most to learn in the new year?

29. List three things you did in the past year you had never done before:

1.

2.

3.

30. What was the best piece of advice someone gave you in the past year?

31. Name your three favorite movies in the past year:

1.

2.

3.

32. If someone hadn't seen you in the past year, what is the biggest change in you they would notice?

33. What do you expect will be the biggest change you will undergo in the new year?

34. If you had the power, what would you most like to change about your life in the new year?

35. What were you proudest of accomplishing in the past year?

36. On a scale of 1 to 10, how excited are you about your prospects for the new year?

37. Name three people you would like to call to wish a Happy New Year.

1.

2.

3.

38. Name something enjoyable you are willing and able to buy for yourself or do for yourself in the first few weeks of the new year.

39. Circle the areas you would most like to see improved or expanded in the new year.

SCHOOL   FRIENDSHIP   WORK

CREATIVITY   HEALTH   MONEY   FAMILY

40. Up to this moment, what do you feel you've gotten out of answering these questions?

This review is a chance to reaffirm for yourself where you've been, where you're going, and how you feel about that. You are unique and special. There is no other person on the planet who would have answered these forty questions exactly as you have answered them. Use your answers as a roadmap for the new year. Allow them to stimulate your creative imagination. Understand what your desires and priorities are for the new year. Knowing where you want to go will help you get there.

THE SUCCESSES OF MY LIFE

PURPOSE

1. To acknowledge oneself for successes.

2. To project future successes.

3. To create the framework for goal setting.

PROCEDURE

1. Complete the activity sheet.

2. Divide students into 6 small groups. Assign each group an age range. In 3 minute rounds have the groups share their successes at that age. Then rotate age ranges and repeat. Continue until all groups have done all 6 ranges.

OPTIONS

Have students share in large group through "popcorn sharing". When a student wants to share they stand up and say the success they had (will have) and that age (i.e.; "At 8, I won the local dog show with my pet poodle.") then they sit down and the next student pops up.

DISCUSSION

A discussion of feelings around success is valuable. Explore feelings of insecurity about being a success, as well as the joys. How do others react to your successes? Your family, friends, etc.?

THE SUCCESSES OF MY LIFE

In each age range, write what you consider to be the greatest successes achieved at that age or hope to achieve when you reach that age.

AGE 5-7

AGE 8-10

AGE 11-13

AGE 14-16

AGE 17-19

AGE 20-25

MAKING THE BEST OF ME | **CHAPTER 5: V-27**

FROM LIMITATION INTO EXPANSION

PURPOSE

1. To explore and identify personal beliefs that limit achievement.

2. To experience moving beyond these beliefs.

PROCEDURE

1. Ask students to complete the Wish List activity sheet.

2. Discuss concepts of limiting beliefs:

   a) PERCEPTION - the way we view ourselves and the world around us. We often tend to block out or filter out any information that does not fit our personal perception.

   b) COMFORT ZONE - the range of behavior in which we feel (mentally and physically) secure operating. When we get out of our comfort zone it feels different and we may, at first, have a hard time coping.

Examples of moving outside one's comfort zone are:

- *a shy student gives an oral book report before his/her class*

- *a basketball player who is used to playing before a crowd of a few hundred fans is in the state finals and playing before a crowd of thousands as well as the television audience*

Change involves looking beyond our perceptions and moving out of our comfort zones.

   c) SELF-TALK - the ways we talk to ourselves to reinforce our perceptions and comfort zones.

3. Have students return to their Wish List and choose one item from any of the five questions.

4. Using this item have the students complete these statements one at a time. Be sure they write the whole sentence each time. Cycle through each statement at least five times before moving to the next statement.

   a) I am worthy of _____, but _____.

   b) I want to _____, but _____.

   c) I am choosing to _____, but _____.

Example: (item from Wish List: better at school)

"I wish I were better at school."

a) I am worthy of doing better at school, but I don't have time.
I am worthy of doing better in school, but I am too dumb, etc. . . . .

b) I want to do better in school, but I don't think I can.
I want to do better in school, but my parents put too much pressure on me, etc.

c) I am choosing to do better in school, but I feel stupid.
I am choosing to do better in school, but I'm afraid I'll lose friends.

5. Now have students write:

"I am choosing to _____."

Example: "I am choosing to do better in school."

Ask the students to write this ten times. Under this, have them write 3-5 ways they can accomplish that. They may want to work together on this section.

DISCUSSION

1. The limiting beliefs that surface after "but" can be explored in class. Students can list their limiting beliefs on the board or charts and discuss how they might expand these perceptions and comfort zones.

2. Take time to check in with the group periodically.

- How are they doing with change?
- Have they noticed their comfort zones expanding?
- Have they noticed their self-talk changing?
- Is it making a difference in their lives? How?

OPTION

A great deal of support can be generated from this exercise. Students can buddy-up and encourage each other in their new risks and behaviors.

FROM LIMITATION INTO EXPANSION | WISH LIST

Complete these sentences. There may be several completions to each sentence.

Date _____

1. What I would like to have different in my life is:

2. I wish I had the ability to:

3. It is not easy for me to:

4. I wish I were better at:

5) I wish I were more motivated to:

THE DATA DUMP

PURPOSE

1. To identify incomplete actions.

2. To initiate a process of completion.

3. To learn how incompletions are limiting.

PROCEDURE

1. Ask students how they feel when they don't finish something they've started. As students give responses, emphasize the limiting nature of incomplete tasks. Indicate that tasks begun (action has been committed to) are stored in the mind under the "To Do" column. When there are too many things "To Do," the mind tends to act overloaded, scattered, lacks motivation and procrastinates. Many times we forget what to do so we won't be able to complete the tasks. This holds energy back from accomplishing what we want to. The result is feeling negatively about ourselves.

2. The first step is to generate the list from our "computer" or our mind. This activity we call the Data Dump. On a piece of paper write down all the incomplete projects, tasks, actions you can think of. If you think of it, write it. Remember, the mind gives no weight or priority to the incomplete task, so anything can surface, from a major task to a trivial task. It's important to list as many incomplete actions as possible. The following list may help trigger your thoughts:

WORK/SCHOOL

- Desk
  - On it . . .
  - In it . . .
  - Around It . . .
- Projects started
- Projects to be started
- Storage
- Follow up
- Reports/Projects
- Planning - Future school plans
- Information you need
- Information someone else needs
- Piece of work you are waiting for
- Materials you're waiting for
- Things you've told someone you're going to do

PERSONAL

- Projects started
- Projects to be started
- Money matters
- Debts/Loans
- Closets
- Clothes
- Shoes
- Cleaning bedroom
- Things to buy
- Bicycle/Automobile
- Outdoors/Yard
- Sports equipment
- Health
- Exercise
- Nutrition
- Doctors, Dentists
- Books to read
- Hobbies

- Community involvement
- Clubs
- Church/Religious involvements
- People to write/call
- Items borrowed/lent
- Feedback to deliver/get

3. In a large group discuss the feelings about doing the Data Dump. Watch for negative judgments and self-talk. Remind students that the purpose is to identify incompletions so they can be completed; not to put themselves down. Notice that we each have lists to do.

4). There are different ways to complete a task. Using the cycle of action (see next activity) determines the steps, but what to do first? Have students look at their lists. With a red or colored pen have them put a line through any activity they have decided not to do. The ones they can let go of (some things are good ideas and never get done, and that's fine; i.e., consciously decide not to complete reading the mystery novel you started during summer vacation.)

5. Now have the students prioritize their remaining items and write them on a new sheet. Next to each item have them write an estimated completion date. Have them be realistic. Suggest not overcommitting. Have them make commitments that can be accomplished.

6. Now the task is to, one at a time, go through the list and complete each task according to the cycle of action.

DISCUSSION

Regular follow-up is important. This can be done in a buddy system or group discussion. Reinforce through discussion the positive feeling and increased energy from the completion process. Also if any feelings of failure arise, take the time to address them.

CYCLE OF ACTION

PURPOSE

1. To teach the elements of a cycle of action.

2. To identify where one gets caught in the cycle.

3. To generate ideas on how to strengthen those areas that are weak in the cycle.

4. To practice active listening.

PROCEDURE

1. Complete the activity sheet "Goal Achieved".

2. Have the students mingle in the room telling each other their responses and moving on to new partners. You can have students walking around doing this or seated in pairs and you tell them to rotate about every two-three minutes.

3. Teach the four steps in a cycle of action. A chart will be helpful for future reference by students. Take examples from students of completed cycles of action in their lives and related feelings.

> **a) Deciding to Take Action.** You decide to commit resources (time, money, people, equipment) to a project. Some people are good at starting things, others are reluctant to commit to taking action.
>
> **b) Doing the Task.** Some people appear to get lost in the doing of a task. They seem to get personal reward in constantly working at a task rather than completing it.
>
> **c) Finishing the Task.** Allowing a task to be completed is easy for some, difficult for others. Some people stop right before they are about to finish. They do not experience the success.
>
> **d) Acknowledging the Completion.** There are two parts to this step. First, you want to acknowledge to yourself that the task is finished and that you are satisfied with the result. Second, you want to get or give acknowledgment. The person who has completed the task wants to know that the result has been seen and the effort appreciated. You may be the person who gives that acknowledgment or the one who receives it. Without acknowledgment, the person who performed the task may feel unappreciated and feel as though the task was without value.

4. Have students get into groups of three and designate them partner A, B, and C.

5. Partner A will begin as speaker, B as active listener, C as observer. They will rotate so each gets a turn in each role.

6. In each round the speaker describes actions, activities, or tasks he/she has not felt complete about. The speaker describes what was done from beginning to end. The active listener clarifies as needed. After 3-5 minutes, the teacher stops them and the observer has 2-3 minutes to give feedback as to what step(s) of the cycle of action the speaker seems to get stuck on. The speaker may want to take notes. Be sure the observer knows what to listen for before the start of the round. Rotate until all students have been in each role.

7. Students then discuss, in their groups, ways they could strengthen the weak areas so they do not get stuck any more.

DISCUSSION

After discussing the meaning and impact of the activity, generate a list on the board or a chart of ideas to strengthen particular weak points.

OPTION

Ask students to commit to using at least one idea with an upcoming task over the next week. After a week, check in with the class. They can return to their small groups and share the results of their experiment or share in the large group. Continue to reinforce the students' awareness regarding completion of the cycle of action.

CYCLE OF ACTION | GOAL ACHIEVED

State a goal that you achieved that was important to you, and then answer the questions below.

My goal was _____.

1. What were the steps you took to achieve your goal?

2. What was the easiest step?

3. What was the hardest step?

4. What did you do to achieve this?

5. Whom did you tell about it?

How did they respond?

6. How did you feel when you achieved your goal?

MAGNIFICENCE

PURPOSE

1. To acknowledge one's positive qualities.

2. To promote an understanding of what it takes to be magnificent.

3. To enhance group cohesiveness and sharing.

PROCEDURE

1. Ask the group, "What is magnificence?"

2. Ask the group, "What actions, deeds, or accomplishments have you done in your life that are magnificent?"

3. Ask the group, "What qualities do you have that enabled you to do these magnificent actions?" Write these qualities on one side of the board, or on a chart titled, "Qualities I Have."

4. Have the students divide into small groups of 6 or 8 students. Be sure each group has an even number (join in if you need to).

5. Ask each group to discuss and share what accomplishments or actions each individual would like to make in the future, which if done the way they'd like, would be "magnificent." Give each group 5-10 minutes.

6. Now ask each group to make a list of the qualities they would need to have in order to accomplish these actions. Give each group 5 minutes.

7. In the large group, record the qualities the groups generated on the opposite side of the board or another chart titled, "Qualities I Would Need to Have."

8. Note the similarity between the two lists. What does this indicate? Elicit the response that they already have the necessary qualities. Indicate that magnificent deeds are done by ordinary people doing extraordinary things. That is what makes us all magnificent. The question becomes, how to activate and utilize these qualities that we already have so that we can do the magnificent things we want to do.

9. This part can be done as a guided imagery or a thinking exercise, whichever you and the students are most comfortable doing. Have the students think of a time when they were really happy because of something they accomplished . . . a time when their magnificence shone through . . . a time when they felt proud of themselves and good about who they were. Suggest that it may be a sports achievement, a time when they got a great report card, or perhaps a time when they did something for someone else.

(If you are doing this as guided imagery, don't have the students write at this point, only bring to mind these qualities, they can write them down later.) Ask them to write the qualities they manifested at that time that allowed and supported this WIN in their lives (i.e., patience, strength, determination, courage, listening, and joyfulness). Now, ask them to think of a situation in their present day lives that is not working as well as they would like (i.e., a relationship with a girlfriend or boyfriend, a class, a job). Ask them to think of how they react in that situation, what happens, who is involved.

Now, once again ask them to focus on the positive qualities they have that can assist them in creating wins in their lives. Then gently have them bring their attention back to the room.

10. Have students choose a partner from their small group. Pick a partner A and B.

11. Partner A will begin. He/She will share the positive qualities he/she possesses which would assist in creating wins in life if used to their fullest. Give 3 minutes. Switch to Partner B for 3 minutes.

12. Now partner A shares the situation that is presently not working in life. Be as specific as you feel comfortable being, the more specific the more powerful the activity. Once they have shared the situation partner B asks, "How could you use the positive qualities you just described to me to change that situation into a win?" Partner A responds. Give 3-5 minutes for this depending on the need. Then switch roles.

13. Partner A and B then take turns, back and forth, completing this sentence, "The Magnificent thing about me is . . ." Give 2-3 minutes.

DISCUSSION

Ask for students to share about the activity.

1. What were their feelings?

2. What did they learn about themselves?

3. Do they feel more capable of being magnificent now?

4. Did it feel silly to say the last sentence completion?

5. Why do you think it is so difficult or uncomfortable for people to acknowledge how wonderful they are?

6. How might it affect life in general if people were more used to and willing to acknowledge their own magnificence? Are they willing to do more of that with each other?

CREATIVE VISUALIZATIONS

PURPOSE

1. To develop an appreciation for the value of creative visualizations.

2. To learn and practice the principles for creative visualizations.

PROCEDURE

1. Have the class read and discuss the introductory information on the activity sheet.

2. Have the class go ahead and fill out the activity sheet and practice their personal visualizations.

3. Have the students all practice their personal visualizations at the same time. Guide them through it. ("Everyone read the first item on your list. Now everyone, close your eyes and have your personal visualization of that come alive inside of you." After thirty seconds, ask them to open their eyes, read their next item and continue on.)

DISCUSSION

1. How many of you were uncomfortable closing your eyes with everyone here? (Ask for raised hands.) How many of you were concerned about looking silly in front of others? (Raised hands.) Discuss how your fear of people's opinion can hold you back.

2. How many of you saw, more than heard, your visualization? Felt it more without seeing it? Review that there is no wrong way to perceive during visualizations. Even drifting off onto other ideas is okay.

3. What creative ways can you use visualizations regularly? Examples are:

   a) Before getting out of bed in the morning, visualize the best for the day.

   b) Before tests or an athletic event, visualize the best performance and excellent results.

   c) Before a meeting with a friend, family member, or teacher that you are concerned about, visualize yourself confident, honest, accepting, etc.

OPTIONS

1. Use visualizations regularly in the class. Have yourself or students lead the group. Have them choose background music (contemporary and calming) if they'd like.

2. Students can write their own scripts for visualizations and take turns leading the class through their visualizations.

    Possible topics:

    • My ideal day

    • My life six months from now, one year from now, five years from now, etc.

    • Being the ideal student/friend

    • Being a winner (sports, an exam, a performance, etc.)

3. Students can record their visualizations on their phone and listen to it on their own. Good times for listening are right before getting out of bed in the morning or prior to drifting off to sleep.

4. Visualizations work excellently in combination with affirmations. Try reviewing and integrating the earlier activities on affirmations. Have students choose one or more of their ten "have-do-be's" and write an affirmation that supports it. (i.e., "I am enjoying listening to music on my new phone.") Have them practice visualizing their "have-do-be's."

CREATIVE VISUALIZATIONS

Creative visualization is the technique of using the inner screen of your mind to create what you want in your life. You are already using creative visualization every day, every minute in fact. It is something you do naturally. It is different than idle daydreaming. It is having your daydreams work for you!

Close your eyes and picture a giant ice cream sundae, complete with whipped cream, chocolate sauce, and nuts. Now feel the cold on your tongue as you put a large spoonful in your mouth and smell the chocolate in the sauce. Now open your eyes.

You see creative visualization is easy and natural. It's also a powerful tool to help you create the kind of life you want. To use creative visualization, there are some easy steps to follow:

1. Decide clearly what you want to create that is positive. It may be to get along better with a friend or your parents, to get an "A" on a test, or hit a home run on the baseball field.

2. Close your eyes and take some slow deep breaths.

3. Call to mind a picture of what you want. See the colors clearly. Feel what is going on. Hear the sounds. Make it a happy, exciting event.

4. Repeat the visualization often with positive energy, attitude and thought.

On the following list, write ten things that you want to "have", or you want to "do", or you want to "be" more in your life. Any combination of ten is fine (three "haves", four "dos", three "bes"). They can be material items or situations (i.e., having new clothes, having new phone, or going to college) or they can be inner experiences (i.e., being more confident, feeling more relaxed, or being more understanding of others).

Write things that are important to you. Then go back over your list and read the first one. Next, close your eyes for about 30 seconds and practice visualizing that first thing coming true. Use all of your senses as much as possible. See what it looks like—how you look with it, doing it, being it. Who is with you? How do you feel? Is there a smile on your face? What would you be saying out loud when it comes true? Let all the details come alive in your imagination. Then go ahead and do this short 30 second visualization for each of the ten things you wrote. Have them come alive inside of you. Practice this often! The more you practice seeing, feeling, hearing, and focusing on what you want, the more you will get it!

THINGS I WANT TO "HAVE", "DO", OR "BE".

Example:

I want to have a new black winter jacket.
I want to do more practicing on my guitar.
I want to be more confident with girls (or boys).

1.

2.

3.

4.

5.

6.

7.

8.

9.

10.

IDEAL SCENE

PURPOSE

1. To explore the creative possibilities for their life's ideal scene.

2. To set the foundation for creation of goals.

PROCEDURE

Do activity sheet and share in small groups.

IDEAL SCENE

What is your ideal scene? If you could snap your fingers, what would your life look like, sound like and feel like?

For each section below write or draw your ideal scene. Allow yourself to be honest and write the picture of your life the way you'd like it to be.

1. Relationship with friends

2. Family and home life

3. School

4. Health and fitness
(Physically, mentally, emotionally)

5. Self image
(What you think and feel about yourself?)

6. Social life

7. Money and finances

8. Free time *(Hobbies, fun, leisure activities)*

9. Work, business, career

10. Service to others/helping in the community

MIND MAPPING

PURPOSE

1. To develop greater creative problem-solving skills.

2. To create a visual overview of aspects of a project by learning mind mapping.

PROCEDURE

1. Review with students the introductory portion of the Mind Mapping activity sheet. Clarify any questions. Reinforce the idea that mind mapping is not a definitive action plan. It is a tool for sparking and inspiring a free association of ideas and possibilities.

2. Before they begin the activity itself, have students share some of the topics they are choosing to mind map.

DISCUSSION

1. What did you learn from doing mind mapping?

2. Did you uncover more ideas and possibilities than you originally thought?

3. What other projects, concerns, or goals current in your life today could you use mind mapping for?

OPTIONS

1. Have students who mind mapped either similar or the same topic (i.e., buying things, getting a part-time job, etc.) form a group and pool all of their ideas together onto one mind map.

2. Divide the class into small groups and have them each mind map the same topic or have them mind map different parts of one topic. Share with the entire class. Use it for historical review, mathematical/science problem-solving, or for group project planning.

3. Use as a supplement for setting up class projects.

MIND MAPPING

Are there ever times when you have many great ideas on how to get something done? Are there also times when you feel stuck with few thoughts on how to handle a situation or a project? Mind mapping is an effective and enjoyable technique for stirring your creative ideas. It is fun, easy, and a valuable skill to know. Mind maps are easy to do because each person makes one up based on their own ideas. Usually your mind works by association, calling up bits and pieces of information in a seemingly illogical sequence. For instance, if someone says "trees" you might think of "green" or "leaves" or "shade" or "apples" or . . . . Each person's brain associates differently. Mind mapping lets you use the freedom of your thoughts and associations to generate ideas that lead to solutions.

Here's how a mind map for buying a new phone might look:

Step 1: Draw a circle and write the topic inside like this:

Step 2: As you think of all the ideas that go with buying a new phone, write them down like this:

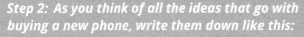
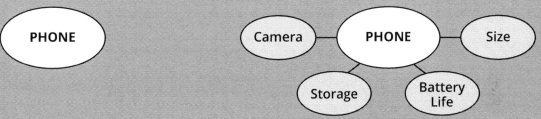

Step 3: As you think of things to add on, fit them with whatever words they seem to go with:

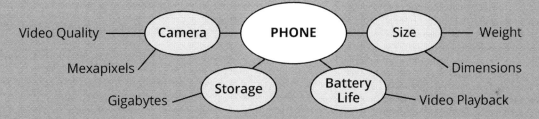

As you do a mind map, what will probably happen is that more thoughts and ideas spring to mind. Just write them down wherever they seem to fit onto the mind map.

A mind map can always have your ideas added on to it. The more you use mind maps, the easier they become. Give yourself time to build this new positive habit. Like all skills, it takes time to learn it. However, using our mind is something we do naturally!

You can use mind maps in as many situations as you want to! For example:

1. Solving a problem (i.e., how to save enough money for a vacation)
2. Thinking of ways to get a job done (i.e., how to get the term paper written)
3. Sorting out a project (i.e., reorganizing the closet)
4. Simplifying something that seems complicated (i.e., becoming healthy)
5. Planning ways to achieve a goal (i.e., getting accepted at a college)

Go ahead and practice three examples of mind mapping. Choose three goals, projects, problems, etc. that right now you would like to act on. Taking out some paper and using the steps outlined, go ahead and create a mind map for each of them.

GOAL SETTING: PART 1
(GUIDELINES)

PURPOSE

1. To learn clear and practical rules for setting goals.

2. To reinforce the value of goal setting.

PROCEDURE

1. Review the introductory section on the activity sheet with the students.

2. Discuss examples from their lives when they accomplished what they set out for. Reinforce that it wasn't an "accident" or "just luck" that they were successful. Have them start to discuss what they did to set up a strong intention within themselves to go after their clear goal.

3. Summarize and give examples of the four guidelines for goal-setting. Make up some typical goals and ask the students if they fulfill the four guidelines.

4. Instruct the students to fill in the chart.

DISCUSSION

1. Who is really in charge of the goals you select?

2. Did you find one of the four guidelines that you need to pay most attention to?

3. What did you learn about yourself and your goals?

OPTIONS

After they have completed the chart, have students pair off. Have partners discuss as to whether the stated goals are desirable, clear, controllable, and achievable. Let it be okay if there are some goals that students wish to keep private and not share.

GOAL SETTING: PART 1
(GUIDELINES)

What are some of the things that you want to do in your life . . . fly a plane, be an entertainer, discover a cure to cancer, play in the World Series? Your life is yours for the making. You can have your dreams come true! It is up to you. If you don't decide where you want to go, you will probably never get there.

You may find yourself going around in circles and not feeling good about what you are doing. Ask yourself what is it you want to do better. What do you want to have? What do you want to achieve? What do you want your life to be like? Sometimes the hardest part of getting what you want is just figuring out what you really want. Once you know what you really want and you are willing to work towards it, you're likely to get it.

The best way to build a sense of your direction is by setting goals. A goal is like a dream . . . it is like seeing the finish line in a race and running right through it. Goals can be something you set out to accomplish in an hour, a day, week, month, year, or a lifetime. Goals are not meant to be taken "heavily" with a lot of pressure. As you feel or understand the value of a goal, make it important. Goals are there to help you and support you in your true purpose. Start with simple goals . . . goals that you really want. Later on you can make goals that are more challenging.

Guidelines for setting goals:

1. Make your goals desirable - It is something that you really want. It really means something to you. Your goal should make you feel good, excited, expanded, and challenged. It should be beneficial to you and in no way harmful to others.

2. Clear - Know exactly what it is that you want. Use your imagination and get a clear and specific picture of it.

3. Controllable - You should be able to control your goal. For example, a controllable goal would be, "I am asking John out to the movies this Saturday," because you can control whether you invite John or not. A goal you can not control would be, "John is going to have to go to the movies on Saturday with me," because he might refuse.

4. Achievable - Goals are to be challenging and also within your reach. For example, "Raising all my grades from "D's" to "A's" in one day," is setting yourself up to lose at your goal. Make it something you can win at.

GUIDELINES

Make a list of five goals that you have. Choose at least one for school, one for friendship, and one for the family. Then review each goal and place a check if it is *desirable* **(D)**, *clear* **(CL)**, *controllable* **(CO)**, and *achievable* **(A)**.

GOALS	D	CL	CO	A
1.	☐	☐	☐	☐
2.	☐	☐	☐	☐
3.	☐	☐	☐	☐
4.	☐	☐	☐	☐
5.	☐	☐	☐	☐

*If any goal does not have all the categories checked, go back and rewrite the goal or cross it off your list.

GOAL SETTING: PART 2
(ACTION PLAN)

PURPOSE

1. To practice developing and using an action plan to accomplish goals.

2. To make a project easier to manage and complete.

PROCEDURE

1. This activity is based on the principles developed in Goal Setting Part 1 - Guidelines.

2. Review the introductory material and discuss examples of action steps for a hypothetical goal or project.

3. Go over the use of the Action Plan Sheet.

4. Students can work individually or in groups assisting one another in developing their action plans. It is helpful to have them choose a goal/project that they have already been working on in the earlier activities in the chapter.

DISCUSSION

1. Is your goal/project more understandable now than before?

2. Who can support you as you take action?

3. How can you support yourself as you take action?

4. How often do you need to review your action plan to see if you are "on course"?

OPTIONS

Practice filling in an Action Plan from the end (result) and working backwards (first step). This approach, called "end results thinking" allows for clearer determination of when steps are due to be completed.

GOAL SETTING: PART 2
(ACTION PLAN)

Once you have chosen a goal for yourself and have checked to see that it "passes" the four guidelines for goal setting, it's time to prepare a plan of action.

Action is important. You can think all you want about scoring the winning basket, but until you go on the court and pick up the ball, nothing can happen. In order to prepare yourself to act wisely in achieving your goal, it's important to prepare an action plan. An action plan is a step by step approach for completing a goal. The action steps can often be developed from ideas on the mind map for that particular goal.

On the activity sheet, go ahead and develop your action plan for a goal you desire. This is your strategy for reaching your goal. Be honest and set due dates that are achievable. Review your action plan often, you may need to add or delete steps as you go. Once you've completed your written plan . . . remember take ACTION and BEGIN!

ACTION PLAN

My goal/project is:

My action steps are: Due by (date):   Completed on:

1.

2.

3.

4.

5.

6.

7.

8.

Notes or reminders:

I completed my goal/project on _____ .

"I acknowledge myself for another success!"

DAILY GOALS

PURPOSE

1. To experience setting and evaluating progress on short-term goals.

2. To build a winning habit in regards to goals.

PROCEDURE

1. Review the guidelines for Goal Setting with students.

2. Have students choose a daily goal they wish to accomplish and fill in the first day of their chart.

3. Each day take a few minutes to discuss their progress.

DISCUSSION

1. How do you feel about your progress on your daily goal(s)?

2. If you didn't achieve your goal, what did you learn about yourself? *(i.e., do you procrastinate, overcommit, choose goals without much desire for it, etc.?)*

3. If you did achieve your goal, what did you learn about yourself?

OPTIONS

1. Do this as a regular weekly activity.

2. Students can practice acknowledgment and self-forgiveness activities to deal with how they are feeling about their progress.

DAILY GOALS

Every day for a week, list one goal you want and are willing to achieve that day. At the end of the day, or first thing the next morning, rate yourself on how well you think you accomplished your goal. Also, include any tips, if you have them, for how you could do it better next time.

Daily Goals	Not Achieved	Partially Achieved	Fully Achieved	Tips
Example: To finish my science report	☐	✓	☐	Watch less TV and start earlier
Monday:	☐	☐	☐	
Tuesday:	☐	☐	☐	
Wednesday:	☐	☐	☐	
Thursday:	☐	☐	☐	
Friday:	☐	☐	☐	
Saturday:	☐	☐	☐	
Sunday:	☐	☐	☐	

At the end of the week, complete these questions:

1. Did the process of setting daily goals make you feel good or frustrated?

2. Do you think the goals helped you accomplish things you might not have accomplished otherwise? Explain:

WEEKLY PLANNER

PURPOSE

1. To keep track of daily assignments and tasks.

2. To develop a system that supports keeping agreements and increased personal responsibility for getting things done on time.

PROCEDURE

1. Discuss the value of keeping a weekly planner or calendar.

2. Review the activity sheet and have the students fill it in.

3. Take time regularly to check in with the students' use of the Weekly Planner.

4. Have students share their progress on their use of their Weekly Planner.

DISCUSSION

1. What does it mean:

- "People write things down not to remember them, but so they don't have to remember them."

- "With self-discipline comes freedom."

2. How do you feel about using your Weekly Planner?

OPTIONS

1. Have students create a special section in their handbook for weekly planners.

2. Start off each week with class time to prepare their Weekly Planner for the coming week. Build that habit of regular planning.

3. Give the students a month's worth of Weekly Planners so they can learn to plan ahead on projects and activities.

WEEKLY PLANNER

Keeping a calendar or list of weekly activities is one way to stay on track. At the end of each week (or at the very beginning of the new week), take time to write out your activities for the upcoming week. Also include your daily school assignments. The Weekly Planner can work only if you use it and refer to it each day. Choose regular times each day to look at, and add onto your weekly planner. Before leaving for school in the morning, after returning home each day, and before going to sleep are times that can work well.

Keeping track of your activities, keeping your agreements, and getting things done are some of the best ways to build your self-esteem.

Go ahead now and, on the next page, create a Weekly Planner for this week.

WEEKLY PLANNER

Week of:	Monday	Tuesday	Wednesday	Thursday	Friday	Saturday	Sunday
Homework *(Which Subjects)*							
Ongoing Projects							
After-School Activities							
Chores *(my room, pets, dishes, etc.)*							
Family Events							
Fun, Friends, Social Activities							
Other							

SIX STEPS TO ACHIEVING EXCELLENCE

PURPOSE

1. To summarize and review the techniques already learned for achieving a goal with excellence.

2. To practice a clear step by step approach for creating success.

PROCEDURE

1. The preliminary activities in the chapter, particularly the activities that teach the first four elements of the Six Steps - ideal scene, mind mapping, goal setting guidelines and action plan, are prerequisites for this activity. If the students need any refreshing on these elements, take the time to review.

2. Read and discuss the Six Steps to Achieving Excellence. Each step builds on the previous one. Review with the class how a "sample" goal would move through each of the steps.

3. Designate a certain amount of time (minimum being one week and maximum being three months) for each student to complete the activity of choosing one goal and achieving it using the Six Steps. Choose time regularly (daily or weekly) for students to work on their steps. Review with them as they progress to see which step different students need assistance on. They can often work in small groups or with partners to review their progress.

4. If any student chooses a goal that would take longer to accomplish than the designated time, "chunk" it down with them (i.e., The goal is to raise a history grade from a "C" to an "A" by year's end. If the time period for the project is sooner, the goal could become - to average a "B" by the end of the allotted time period).

5. Review each step with the students. If their goal doesn't "pass" step 3 (Guidelines) no matter how much good intention, planning, and action, it will likely not succeed (i.e., a goal of losing 40 pounds in 3 weeks wouldn't pass the guidelines of achievability).

6. Take on a goal along with them.

7. Encouragement and class discussion of "stuck points" and "mini-wins" along the way to completion is very helpful.

8. Weave in affirmations, creative visualizations, acknowledgment activities, as ways to keep them focusing positively on their goals.

DISCUSSION

1. What have you learned about setting a goal and accomplishing it?

2. Which step(s) for you was the easiest? Which was the most challenging?

3. Were there people who assisted you along the way? Who? How?

4. If you could improve your skill for reaching your goal for next time, what would you do differently?

SIX STEPS TO ACHIEVING EXCELLENCE

You have learned many of the skills for reaching your goals and achieving what you want. Now it's time to put it all together. Achieving excellence is a six step approach. In this chapter you have already learned most of these steps.

STEPS TO ACHIEVING EXCELLENCE

STEP ONE: In your imagination (using creative visualization) create an *IDEAL SCENE* of exactly what you want to accomplish.

STEP TWO: Using the hopes and dreams from your *IDEAL SCENE* write a *MIND MAP* letting all the ideas and possibilities come alive.

STEP THREE: State your goal clearly and review it using the *GOAL SETTING GUIDELINES*.

STEP FOUR: Write your *ACTION PLAN* outlining the specific steps that you can take to achieve your goal.

STEP FIVE: *TAKE ACTION!* Doing does it. Start and get involved. Learn from any mistakes and get back on course.

STEP SIX: *ACKNOWLEDGE* yourself for doing great and accomplishing your goal. Thank others for supporting you.

1. Create your Ideal Scene.

2. Draw your Mind Map.

3. Review Goal Setting Guidelines.

4. Prepare your Action Plan.

5. Carry out the action. DO IT!

6. Give thanks. Acknowledge yourself and others.

As you participate in each of the six steps, you will be heading for success.

Take the time now, to begin to practice the Six Steps to Achieving Excellence. Using all that you have learned in this chapter and the Six Step approach, your extended activity will be to choose one goal, project, or task that you truly want to accomplish and go forward and achieve it. This may take a week, a month, or more to complete. Discuss with your teacher the time period and suggestions for your particular project of achieving what you want using the Six Steps Approach. Have fun and know that you can do it!

MANAGING MONEY

PURPOSE

1. To examine personal attitudes about money.

2. To identify strategies to create more positive attitudes and behaviors regarding money.

3. To identify the importance of money in one's life.

PROCEDURE

See activity sheet for instructions.

NOTE: It is helpful for the teacher to complete a form with the students.

DISCUSSION

1. Discuss the answers to the questions on the sheet.

2. Examine the attitudes and concerns that come up.

3. Explore the importance of family attitudes about money.

4. Have students share money making ideas and goals.

5. Be aware of emotions that may surface and bring them to the students' attention.

MANAGING MONEY

Take a few minutes to fill out this form. As you do, be honest with yourself. Notice the feelings that come up as you think about money.

1. Things I need money for (weekly):

2. Things I need money for (long term):

3. I waste money by:

4. Ways I can be more careful with money are:

5. The feelings I have about money are:

6. My family's attitude about money is:

7. The way I'd like to think about money is:

8. The things that stop me from saving money are:

9. I can change this by:

10. The reasons money is so important to me are:

11. Ways I can earn money:

12. I'm saving money for:

13. I can save money by:

14. My goal is to save $_____ by (date) _____.

To do this I will follow this plan:

TREASURE MAPS

PURPOSE

To reinforce, through a collage activity, the ability to choose a positive focus and create desired results.

PROCEDURE

A treasure map is a physical picture representing a person's ideal reality. It allows people to form a sharp and positive image of what they want to create. The project is to make a "treasure map" on light cardboard or tag board, by cutting out pictures and words from magazines and pasting them on the chart. Drawings, pictures and lettering can be included too. The idea is to make the entire treasure map a picture collage of what they want more of in their lives.

Students can have a general focus of what they want more of in their lives or the focus can be more specific (i.e., their friendships, future career, hobbies, family, world peace, success, travel, health, etc.). Some suggestions in creating treasure maps are:

>   1. Be sure to put yourself in the treasure map. Using a photograph of yourself works great. If not, draw yourself in.
>
>   2. Only include positive and affirming pictures.
>
>   3. Put an affirmation on it: "I love driving my new racing bike."
>
>   4. Make it colorful, creative, and fun.

DISCUSSION

1. Did you notice if some of your "dreams for the future" were similar to others? How so?

2. What does this statement mean: "What we focus on, we tend to create."

3. How did you feel describing your treasure map as if it already is happening? *(Use this question if you do Option #1.)*

OPTIONS

1. Have students share their completed treasure maps with the class. Students can hold it up while they talk about it. Have them share as if it's already happened (i.e., "I am having a great time camping. And here I am wearing my new clothes, as I am spending time having fun with my friends.") Give each student 2-3 minutes to describe their treasure map, acting as if it has already happened. Use "I am . . ." statements.

2. Have the class together create a group treasure map on a topic that they are concerned with (i.e., solutions to world hunger, world peace, housing the homeless). Keep the focus on a positive solution.

THE WEEK IN REVIEW - 1

PURPOSE

1. To provide a tool to increase the awareness of the week's activities, thoughts and feelings.

2. To provide a tool to identify areas of growth or improvement.

PROCEDURE

Have students fill out the form at the end of each week.

DISCUSSION

Periodic discussion on students' progress, procrastination and growth is helpful. Be sure the discussion is supportive in nature. The group can work together to assist students who seem to be stuck. The importance here is to acknowledge successes (even small ones) in oneself and in others, to work on recurrent stuck areas and not to make anyone wrong for their rate of progress or feelings. As acceptance and support for one another grows, greater trust can develop.

THE WEEK IN REVIEW - 1

1. What was the highlight of this week for you?

2. Was there a person you got to know better or appreciate more this week?

In what way?

3. What was the major thing you learned about yourself this week?

4. Did you procrastinate (put things off) this week?

If you did, what things did you put off?

How can you follow up on these things next week?

5. Identify three decisions or choices you made this week and the results of the choices.

    1.

    2.

    3.

6. In general, how did the week go for you?

7. Is there anything you need to clear up or complete so you can start next week fresh? (example: apologize to a friend, complete a school assignment, etc.)

8. What might you do to make things go well next week?

    1.

    2.

    3.

    4.

    5.

THE WEEK IN REVIEW - 2

PURPOSE

1. To give each person an opportunity to reflect on the past week.

2. To increase communication skills and sharing.

3. To build group trust.

PROCEDURE

1. This is an alternate activity to "The Week In Review." You may want to trade off weekly.

2. Ask participants to form partnerships or triads.

3. Have students pick who will go first, second, third. The person to the right of the one being interviewed will ask the questions. It is everyone's job to listen attentively and non-judgmentally. No discussion.

4. Give each person five minutes to be interviewed. Then you switch them. Tell students to make up their own questions if they finish early.

5. Example questions:

    1. "What new and good things happened to you this past week?"

    2. "What was challenging about your week?"

    3. "Is there something you meant to do this week but put off? What?"

    4. "What one thing did you do that you enjoyed?"

    5. "What can you do to make next week a good one?"

    6. "Is there anything you need assistance with? What?"

    7. "Is there anyone who can assist you? Who?"

CHAPTER 6

Reaching Out to Your Family and Community

TEACHING TIPS & SUGGESTIONS

1 Encourage the family's active involvement and support. Often, this is a challenge. The more you can inspire the parents to share in the commitment to their child's enhanced self-esteem, the more impact can be made. In many of the activities in the chapter, parents and other family members are invited to participate. Parents are often grateful for having their children involve them in these family building activities.

2 We suggest you write or call each parent at the start of the course to explain the nature and benefits of the class. Also encourage their at home support of their child and involvement in the family-oriented activities.

3 Respect the uniqueness of each student's family. Since family situations are so different, it may be necessary to adapt some of the activities to honor the particular dynamics of any family. A grandmother, an older sister, or a brother can easily fill in as the parent figure, if necessary. Accepting and acknowledging each person's family, as they are, is essential.

4 Communicate often with the parents. Sending "good news" notes home and making "good news" phone calls can be a refreshing change from the typical negative progress reports or notices.

5 Consider hosting class "Family Nights" where your students and their families come together. These nights can be strictly social in nature, or be structured to introduce several of the communication and rapport-building activities. Your students and you can take an active part in promoting these nights as fun and educational gatherings for family skills development.

6 Find ways for students to experience themselves as contributing members of their community. Bridging the gap between school and the "real world" is important. Invite community leaders and local people, who exemplify a lifestyle of high achievement and a commitment to personal and social responsibility, to come as guest speakers. Provide students with opportunities to give back to others through community "service" projects. These activities let students see that as they share themselves, they can make a great contribution in others' lives. Knowing that they can make a significant difference in another's life is an extremely fulfilling and a powerful self-esteem booster.

ACTIVITY PREVIEWS

FAMILY POSITIONS EVERYONE!
Focus: Patterns of family dynamics.
Time: 20-30 minutes

FAMILY DYNAMICS
Focus: Partnership activity examining family dynamics.
Time: 30-40 minutes

HEART TO HEART
Focus: Practice expressing specific appreciation to family members.
Time: 1st session - 25 minutes;
2nd session - 15 minutes
Activity: Page VI-07

APPRECIATION LETTER
Focus: Writing a letter to your parents expressing appreciation.
Time: 15-20 minutes
Activity: Page VI-09

STRENGTH CIRCLES
Focus: Fun, interactive activity acknowledging your own and others' strengths
Time: 20-30 minutes
Activity: Page VI-11

WHAT IF I WERE A PARENT?
Focus: Through role reversal, examine parenting from a parent's point of view.
Time: 30-50 minutes
Activity: Page VI-13

FAMILY TALK
Focus: Caring feedback with family members.
Time: Varies - out of class
Activity: Page VI-15

LETTER OF ACKNOWLEDGMENT
Focus: Express pride in yourself to your parents.
Time: 20-30 minutes
Activity: Page VI-17

CONNECTING WITH FAMILY: ACTIVITIES
Focus: Selection of activities to do at home to enhance family relationships.
Time: Varies - out of class
Activity: Page VI-19

"MAKE MY DAY"
Focus: Ideas to brighten someone else's day.
Time: Varies - Out of class
Activity: Page VI-21

KEYS TO HAPPINESS
Focus: Interviews outside of class to increase awareness of ways to achieve happiness.
Time: 30 minutes (to discuss findings)
Activity: Page VI-23

WHAT CAN I GIVE?
Focus: Exploring what I can give to others and how.
Time: 30 minutes
Activity: Page VI-25

MAKING A DIFFERENCE: SERVICE
Focus: Experience being of service in the world and the feelings that result.
Time: Varies
Activity: Page VI-27

FAMILY POSITIONS EVERYONE!

PURPOSE

1. To build group cohesiveness.

2. To promote awareness of how other family members feel.

PROCEDURE

1. Ask students to form groups in different parts of the room according to their birth position in their family: eldest, youngest, in-betweens, only child.

2. Have students share with other members of their group:

   - *How does it feel to be (an only child, eldest, etc.?)*
   - *What responsibilities did you have?*
   - *What advantages did you have?*
   - *Did you like it?*
   - *Which position were you jealous of, if any?*
   - *What were some of your feelings, about older/younger siblings?*
   - *What role did you play in the family (protector, responsible)?*

3. Have two groups join together. (Mix groups together whichever way you want).

4. Now ask these groups to share about:

   - *Who did you think had more power in the family?*
   - *How did you feel toward siblings?*
   - *Who got attention in your family and how did they get it?*

5. Remix groups and continue discussion.

DISCUSSION

1. Did you identify with anyone else in the group?

2. How did you feel being with others in the same birth position as you?

3. Did you feel a common bond with those in the same birth position as you?

4. What did you learn?

5. Can we make generalizations about birth positions?

6. In what way does your birth position and the role you play in your family affect your relationships with other people? (i.e., if you are the big brother in your family, do you choose a role as a "big brother" to your friends?)

FAMILY DYNAMICS

PURPOSE

1. To explore feelings about family.

2. To explore one's place in the family.

PROCEDURE

1. Have students write a paragraph about their family. They can write whatever they want.

2. Put this page aside and have them write a paragraph about their ideal family.

3. On the same page have them write a paragraph about what it would be like to be an orphan.

4. Now go back to the original paragraph. What are the similarities and differences between your family and your ideal family? Is there anything you can do to bring the two closer together?

5. Now have the students write several paragraphs describing how each member of their family, including him/herself, is unique. How do these differences contribute to the family and to the function of the family?

6. Have students partner up. Pick a partner A and a partner B. Partner A will ask partner B the following questions. Cycle through the questions as many times as time allows. You may want to post these. Provide the student with your own personal examples.

   a) What is something you like about your family?

   b) What is something you don't like about your family?

   c) How do you react to that?

   d) How do you feel about your role in that situation?

   e) What could you do to change the situation or your response to it so you feel better and more in charge?

7. After 3-5 minutes, allow a few minutes for partner sharing.

8. Partner B asks partner A the questions. Provide sharing time after 3-5 minutes.

DISCUSSION

Ask students to share about what they discovered in this activity. Be sensitive to the emotions that may surface. Be aware that the dynamics of the family can be confusing, especially for the teenager who is attempting to define his/her own identity. Do not judge what they say. Do your best to understand that they may be in the process of clarifying the issues that may surface in this exercise.

HEART TO HEART

PURPOSE

1. To promote appreciation of one's family and its individual members.

2. To practice positive communication within the family.

PROCEDURE

1. Have students complete the activity sheet.

2. Have students partner up. Pick partner A and B.

3. Partner A will go first and tell partner B what family member they are to represent (Mom, Dad, Uncle, Sister, etc.). Give them the name you usually call that person. Now practice saying your appreciation statement to partner B as if they were that family member. Notice the feelings you have (are you uncomfortable, giggly, etc.). Then partner A moves on to the next person in his/her family and repeats the process. When partner A has completed his/her list, it is partner B's turn. If you finish early, share quietly with your partner.

DISCUSSION

1. Was one family member harder than others to write about? Why?

2. What appreciation statements would they like their family members to tell them?

OPTION

Each student then takes his/her list home and actually tells his/her family members individually the appreciation statements practiced in class.

HEART TO HEART

The many things that make my family special are:

I am grateful to my family for:

For each member of your family, complete the following two sentences. You can use relatives and others as well, if you consider them your family.

Person's Name	What I appreciate about you is:	One way I can show you I care is:

MAKING THE BEST OF ME | **CHAPTER 6: VI-07**

APPRECIATION LETTER

PURPOSE

To express appreciation to parent(s).

PROCEDURE

Students complete activity sheet.

APPRECIATION LETTER

Write a letter to your parent(s). Tell them the things you appreciate about them. Tell them what you have learned from them. This exercise works even when your parents are no longer living or were absent during some part of your life. Let them know how much you care. If you want to mail it or give it to them, you can. Otherwise, it's just for you.

Dear _____,

Love,

_____
         (your name)

STRENGTH CIRCLES

PURPOSE

1. To practice self-acknowledgment.

2. To experience receiving acknowledgment from others.

PROCEDURE

1. Review the activity sheet and instructions with the class.

2. After they have completed the activity at home, review through discussion.

DISCUSSION

1. How did you feel receiving acknowledgment from someone close to you?

2. Did they write or say things about you that surprised you? If so, what?

3. How could doing activities like this one improve your relationship with your family?

OPTIONS

Have the students take extra Strength Circles activity sheets home. Invite them to give one to each family member who can then be the focus of the activity.

STRENGTH CIRCLES

1. Sit down with parent(s), family member(s), or friend and ask them to write "The positive qualities they see in you," in the outer circle.

2. When they are done, ask them to read to you what they wrote and explain to you why they wrote it.

3. Next, complete the Strength Circles by writing any additional positive qualities that you see in yourself in the inner circle. You may also repeat any qualities that were written in the outer circle.

HAVE FUN!

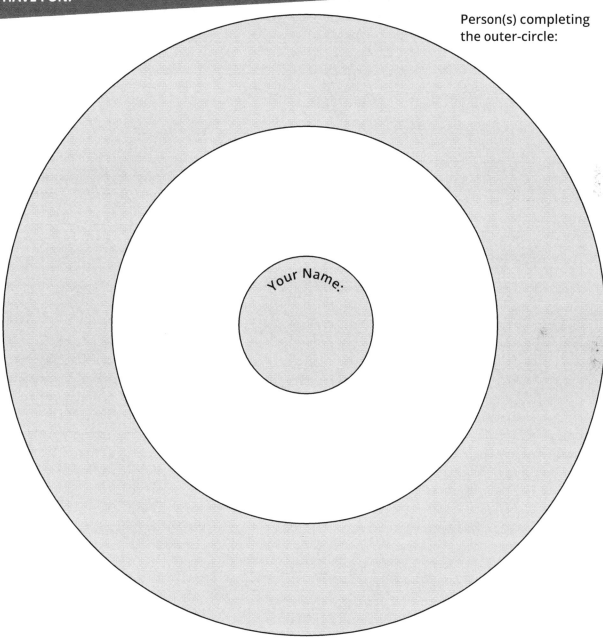

Person(s) completing the outer-circle:

Your Name:

WHAT IF I WERE A PARENT?

PURPOSE

1. To examine how students would parent themselves.

2. To see parenting from the parents' point of view.

PROCEDURE

1. Have students fill out the activity sheet.

2. Choose students to role play various situations from #6 on the activity sheet.

DISCUSSION

1. What was it like role playing a parent?

2. What were the different points of view?

3. How can the gap between children and parents be bridged?

OPTIONS

This activity can be changed slightly to "What if I Were My Teacher?," or "What if I Were My Brother/Sister?"

WHAT IF I WERE A PARENT?

Imagine yourself the parent of your own children.

1. What three sentences of advice would you give to them if they were your age?

a)

b)

c)

2. What three things would you not say to them?

a)

b)

c)

3. What two things would you allow them to do that you are not allowed to do?

a)

b)

4. What two things would you not allow them to do?

a)

b)

5. List five ways in which your children's lives might be different from yours.

a)

b)

c)

d)

e)

6. How would you work with your children to solve the biggest problem you currently have with your parents?

FAMILY TALK

PURPOSE

1. To provide a safe and caring way to give and receive feedback in the family.

2. To enhance family closeness and communication.

PROCEDURE

Review the Activity Sheet with the students. You may want to give students an opportunity to practice this activity in class before bringing it home.

DISCUSSION

Ask students to share their experiences of doing this activity with their families. Students can provide encouragement and support for each other.

FAMILY TALK

Each person will have a chance to complete the following sentences without anyone else saying anything (i.e., agreeing, denying, making comments, etc.) This is a special time to speak what is true for you and not hold back when completing these sentences. Everyone will have a chance to complete all of the following sentences with each family member and then it will be the next person's turn. Remember, feedback is best received when delivered in an honest and loving way. Use this time to share your caring with each other.

1. What I appreciate about you is . . . .

2. What I need more of from you is . . . .

3. What I need less of from you is . . . .

4. What I'd like for us to do less of is . . . .

5. What I'd like for us to do more of is . . . .

6. Something I've never told you is . . . .

7. Something I'd like to hear from you is . . . .

(The person receiving this feedback will now say to the person who delivered the statement what it is they really wanted to hear.)

LETTER OF ACKNOWLEDGMENT

PURPOSE

1. To express pride in self.

2. To communicate accomplishments and reasons for their parent(s) to be proud of them.

3. To build self-confidence.

PROCEDURE

1. See activity sheet for instructions.

2. Students may want to share letters with buddies or small groups before sending them.

DISCUSSION

1. How did it feel to write the letter?

2. What did you learn?

3. How do you think your parents will respond?

4. Can you be proud of yourself regardless of how they respond?

5. How would you like them to respond?

LETTER OF ACKNOWLEDGMENT

Write a letter to your parents to let them know that you are proud of yourself and they have reason to be proud of you and of your accomplishments. Include in your letter what your goals are, why they are important to you and the steps you are going through to accomplish them. Write how you feel about how you are doing and why what you are doing in your life right now is important to you. Also, you may want to express your appreciation and thankfulness to them.

CONNECTING WITH FAMILY: ACTIVITIES

PURPOSE

To present activities to do with the family to create greater connectedness and understanding.

PROCEDURE

On these pages there are several ideas of activities students can do with their families. Students may also brainstorm additional activities. Some teachers find it useful to create mock families in the classroom and have these "families" do the activities before the students bring them home. It is best to allow these activities to be optional.

DISCUSSION

1. Discuss with the students any apprehensions or concerns they may have about introducing these activities to their families.

2. Encourage students to share their experiences with the class after they have done an activity at home. The class can often assist a student if the experience was not what he/she expected as well as share in the excitement of greater communication with family.

CONNECTING WITH FAMILY: ACTIVITIES

A FAMILY JOURNAL

Create a family journal by placing blank paper or a journal book in a special place in the house. Each day, or each week, everyone in the family writes in the journal. Family members can take turns choosing the topic for the week or it can be free form writing. This isn't a place to criticize someone. It is a way to express feelings, thoughts, experiences, impressions, appreciations, etc. with family members. There can be a family meeting to read that week's entries or each person can read them at his/her leisure.

FAMILY NOTES

For the period of a week everyone in the family sends everyone else kind notes. Choose a place to exchange the notes or let the location of the daily notes come as a surprise to the receiver. Be sure to label notes with people's names to avoid confusion. Notes can be simple one liners or a few lines. They are compliments, appreciations, or just plain kind things to say to that person (i.e., "Dinner last night was great." "I loved laughing so hard with you.")

SIMPLE GIFTS

Brainstorm, with your family, types of simple gifts people would like to receive. They can be gifts of time (15 minutes of baseball instruction), gifts of appreciation (10 compliments in one day), or material gifts (homemade or low cost). Write all the ideas on slips of paper and place them in a bowl. Each family member picks a slip and chooses a family member to whom they will give that gift. Within a time period determined by the family (no longer than a week) family members give their gifts.

Be sure to show appreciation when you receive your gift. You can choose new gifts every month or couple of weeks, whatever the family decides. Communicate with each other on how you like the activity. Add new gift ideas to the bowl as you get them. Some families have a bowl out and family members pick slips at random to give to others. Make sure all family members are participating in both the giving and receiving. Have a family discussion if this is not happening.

"MAKE MY DAY"

PURPOSE

1. To give suggestions that would brighten someone's day.

2. To experience doing something for someone that could brighten their day.

PROCEDURE

1. Students read ideas and choose one or more to complete.

2. They may want to share their experiences when the activity is completed.

3. Students can brainstorm additional ideas and add them to the list for future use.

"MAKE MY DAY"

There are many ways to brighten up your own and other people's day. Some ideas are:

1. Write a letter or short note to someone special in your life (grandparents, brother, sister, friend, teacher, et al.) and let them know how much you appreciate them, the things you have learned from them and how much you care. Then mail it.

2. Today, spend at least five minutes in front of the mirror saying positive self talk out loud as you look into your eyes.

3. Today, call or write someone you care about and tell them how grateful you are for their presence in your life.

4. Call someone you admire and look up to. Invite them to lunch, and take time to talk and share with them about the qualities in them you admire.

5. Today, compliment at least three people on how attractive they look.

6. Today, as you go through the day, tell yourself at least three positive compliments.

Add some of your own ideas:

7.

8.

9.

10.

KEYS TO HAPPINESS

PURPOSE

1. To increase awareness of the ability we have to create happiness.

2. To benefit from the wisdom of others.

PROCEDURE

Ask students to do the interviews described on the activity page by a certain date. Lead the class in a discussion of their findings.

DISCUSSION

1. Did you find any similarities in the responses you recorded?

2. Were there material things or items that seemed to produce happiness? (i.e., money, cars, homes, clothes, etc.) Name them. Were there also "inner" or personal experiences that also allowed for happiness? Name some (i.e., kindness, spending time with close friends or family, caring for yourself, etc.)

3. Did you notice some people's happiness had nothing to do with how much they possessed? What attitudes inside a person build happiness?

4. Who is really in charge of your happiness, you or others?

5. Have you used any of the keys people talked to you about?

6. How could you practice your favorite alternatives?

OPTIONS

1. Have students interview people over sixty years old.

2. Have them interview each other in the class.

3. Have students use the concept of leadership instead of happiness. What makes a good leader? Interview leaders in the community, school, etc. and write "Keys for a Good Leader."

KEYS TO HAPPINESS

Interview a few people you think are happy and enjoying their lives. Ask them what they have found to be keys for living a happy life.

Keys for living a happy life:

1.

2.

3.

4.

5.

6.

7.

8.

9.

10.

My favorite keys are:

1.

2.

3.

4.

5.

WHAT CAN I GIVE?

PURPOSE

1. To explore what each person can give in the world and how.

2. To become aware of the feelings and experiences gained by giving.

PROCEDURE

1. See the activity sheet for instructions.

2. Demonstrate how the process is done.

- Partners sit across from one another.
- The listening partner doesn't comment, only supports.
- No need to censor what is being said or to think about it.

3. Tell students when to switch roles.

DISCUSSION

1. Provide a few minutes between partners at the conclusion of the activity for quiet discussion.

2. What experiences were you looking for? Do you usually get them when you give? When? When not?

WHAT CAN I GIVE?

Ask yourself, what is there that you could give to people that would express love, compassion, joy and/or truth? What is it that you could give that can make a difference in someone else's life as well as your own?

Find a partner. One of you will be asking the questions and the other answering them. Cycle through the questions repeatedly. When you come up with the same answer to the last question, that cycle of questions is complete. Beginning with question #1, start again, reviewing another thing you can give. Take about three minutes each, so both of you have the opportunity to answer the questions. If you get stuck, have your partner repeat the question until the next answer comes up.

1. What can you give?

2. How can you give that?

3. What experience are you looking for?

MAKING A DIFFERENCE: SERVICE

PURPOSE

1. To enhance awareness of each individual's power to make a difference.

2. To build group cohesiveness.

PROCEDURE

1. Discuss the concept of service. Define it. (Discuss unconditional giving: giving to give, not to receive; giving from the heart or caring; and it is the thought and feeling behind the gift that counts, not the size).

2. Explore whether students feel they can make a difference in the world around them. Why or why not? Assist students in finding ways in which they already are serving their family, friends, school, and/or community without even knowing it.

3. Have students complete the activity sheet.

4. In small groups or as a large group share world visions. You may want to create a mural depicting the group's world visions, or do "Man/Woman on the Street (or in the Hall)" interviews to gather more world visions. Discuss similarities/differences. Brainstorm ways to bring the world closer to that vision.

5. In small groups or as a large group decide on a way to serve the school or community, make a plan, assign tasks, (i.e., phone calls to nursing homes to see if it is okay to come and spend time with residents), arrange for materials, and do it. (See Project Idea pages.)

6. Share experiences after the completion of the Service Project.

7. The group may decide to commit to doing one act of service each week or each month.

DISCUSSION

1. How did you feel being of service?

2. Do you see more ways that you can make a difference, even by yourself? What are they?

3. What was the response of those you served?

4. What happened in your group as you were of service together?

5. Could you organize your family to do service projects for the community? For each other?

MAKING A DIFFERENCE: SERVICE

1. I can make a difference in my family by:

2. I can make a difference in my school by:

3. I can make a difference in my community by:

4. What is the best you can imagine for the world?

5. One thing you could do this week to bring the world closer to your vision is:

6. Are you willing to do that? (Be honest.)

7. Who could assist you?

MAKING A DIFFERENCE: SERVICE

PROJECT IDEAS

Go out of your way to greet a former enemy with kindness. Don't explain why you are doing this; just be nice to them.

Clean out your closet and house and give away items of clothing, books, etc. that you no longer use or need. Give them to the charity of your choice.

Drop some money into the shopping bag of a stranger at a grocery store. Don't let them see you do it.

Prepare a meal for someone in need and have someone else take it to them. Remain an anonymous friend.

Arrange for a special treat to be delivered to someone at school and do it anonymously.

Send an anonymous gift to someone in a hospital or convalescent home.

Buy two movie tickets and give them to someone anonymously.

Practice making a contribution of money or clothing to a non-profit organization.

One person could take a friend to a movie or entertain him/her while the rest of the group does a good deed for him/her. (One example of such a favor might be to clean the friend's room while he/she is away.)

Contact a local minister or service group and do a service project for a perfect stranger.

Become a "guardian angel" for a friend. Give gifts, cards, etc. anonymously and periodically throughout the year.

Send a present to one of society's servants who aren't often acknowledged—a police officer, a dentist, a politician, a teacher, etc.

At a market, give the checker $1 or $5 and tell them it's to be applied anonymously to the next person's bill.

Drop some change in a public place and leave it for someone else to find.

Leave a thank-you card on the windshield of a police officer's car.

Leave small cloth bags filled with pennies on a playground at an elementary school just before recess.

Pay for a stranger's meal in a restaurant without letting them know you did it.

Once a month send a holiday card or gift to a friend anonymously.

Leave your waiter or waitress a thank-you card in addition to a tip.

Fill up a parking meter.

Go up to person on the street, hand them a dollar and say, "I think you dropped this," and walk away quickly.

Pick up trash that is lying around your neighborhood.

Say nice things about someone you dislike.

Write and send a poem or card to someone. Make sure you don't let them know it's from you.

Give some flowers to someone you care about, but don't let them know the flowers are from you. Then write about how you feel or draw a picture to express your feelings.

Buy something you have been wanting for yourself, and give it away anonymously. How do you feel? What joy do you think your gift might bring them?

Buy a little toy for a brother, a sister, or a friend and hide it in their room. Then see if you can be around when they find it and observe their process. What was their reaction? What experience did they seem to be having? How do you feel about being a giver?

Make a list of at least three ways you could be of service to your family this week. Then do them.

Visit a convalescent or children's hospital. Take flowers to a patient there.

Contact a local church and find out who needs assistance in your community (e.g., a house cleaned, a meal prepared, a room painted, etc.). Choose some way that you can be of service in your community.

Do a service project in your community with others (i.e., clean up a park, a beach, or public place; paint or fix up the home of someone who is in need; etc.).

Select a local organization, church group, school, educational organization, hospital, convalescent home, or service organization and volunteer time on a regular basis (i.e., once a week or more) where you just give and do whatever is needed. Doing service is your reward.

With a friend or family member, make one to twenty sack lunches. Take them to a local park or community area and give them to people who are hungry.

CHAPTER 7
Personal Journal

TEACHING TIPS & SUGGESTIONS

1 Start the journal work within the first two weeks of the term. Present it to the students as something very special. As the students use their journals on a daily and weekly basis, it becomes very vital and rich.

2 Read the entire chapter thoroughly before introducing it to the students.

3 Take the time to privately complete the teacher preparation section before introducing the unit.

4 There are five activities in the Student Journal – Part 1. You may allow five to ten minutes each day, or every few days, for "Reflections" and/or "Honesty Wheel." Students can also be encouraged to make use of the "Reflections" section as frequently as they want. It can become very precious to them.

Allow about ten minutes at the end of each week, or at the very start of the new week, for the "Looking Back Over My Week" activity. Consistency is the key in having your students gain value from these journal activities.

5 Introduce Student Journal – Part 2 as it best suits the framework of your class. You may assign or have the students select a topic each week. Provide ample time for discussion and sharing of their writing.

ACTIVITY PREVIEWS

TEACHER JOURNAL PREPARATION/WORK
Focus: Teacher journal exercises that increase understanding and rapport with students.
Time: Varies

GUIDELINES FOR READING STUDENT JOURNALS
Focus: Keys to make reading journals fun.
Time: Varies

STUDENT JOURNAL - PARTS 1 & 2
Focus: Introspective writing activities to enhance self-awareness and self-esteem.
Time: Varies

MAKING THE BEST OF ME | **CHAPTER 7: VII-03**

TEACHER JOURNAL PREPARATION

It is highly suggested that teachers prepare themselves for implementing journal work by personally completing a sequence of journal topics. By doing preliminary journal work ourselves, we can free emotional blocks and limited thinking so that our responses to our students can be more clear and effective. The goal is to prepare the teacher to respond both to student journal entries and to handle the day-to-day challenges of working with students, with caring and clarity.

Journal preparation allows us to re-enroll in the school of our own personal growth. This is an opportunity to enhance the positive aspects of ourselves and turn our so-called weaknesses into strengths. The goal we have for ourselves here is to develop a system of self-support and to free ourselves from the disturbances inside which may be activated in us by troubled and troublesome students.

The goal in working with students is to show them that someone cares about them no matter how hard they may try to disprove it; and further that this caring is not laden with a lot of victimizing, persecuting or rescuing energy.

GUIDELINES FOR TEACHER JOURNAL PREPARATION

1. Do the sequence in order.

2. Do your journal work in a quiet place free from distractions with plenty of time to complete the assignment. (You may want to play some music.)

3. Let whatever emotion that comes up in your writing be okay. Be honest and accepting of what is present as you write.

4. Journal work doesn't necessarily have to be a heavy experience. You may want to look upon it as a opportunity to lift the weight from your shoulders. It might even be fun and inspiring.

5. Know that your journal work is for your personal benefit, and it will allow you to assist your students in deriving maximum benefit from their journal writing.

TEACHER JOURNAL WORK

TOPICS

1. A LETTER OF SELF-SUPPORT:

Write a letter of loving support from you to that strong, wise part of you which has gotten you though the good times and the tough times. Include memories from childhood which were challenging and which were joyful. Give yourself appreciation for the things you did well and forgiveness and support for the things you were still learning. Remember that "if we knew better, we would probably do better." Put your heart into it.

2. AN IMPORTANT EVENT IN MY LIFE:

(Do one journal entry for each of several significant events. Do them in chronological order.)

Describe an event which really changed your life. It may or may not be one specific moment. It may be a series of moments (i.e., going to college, falling in love, a family vacation, etc.) What happened? Who was involved? How did you feel? What faulty beliefs did you discover you held? What did you gain from the event? What qualities, strengths, and learnings did you discover in yourself? Once we see the value and the positive gain, we begin to see how all challenges can be seen as blessings in disguise.

3. UNFINISHED BUSINESS:

(Do one for each significant person in your life's history.)

Elizabeth Kubler Ross, in her book On Death and Dying, writes about the need for the terminally ill to complete the "unfinished business" which they have with a significant person/people in their lives. We can all benefit from completing the business of our relationships inside ourselves. It may be that you hold some resentment or guilt. It may be simply that you never told someone(s) you love that you love them.

The eventual goal of this process is to heal the memories, forgive, and let go of any judgments, emotions and habits which you may have held onto. The goal is not to change others. It is to return to a place of loving inside yourself.

Write a letter to a significant person in your life sharing your honest feelings and thoughts. This letter is private, and is not necessarily to be shared with the person. Recall specific events in your relationship and share your reaction to them in the letter. You may find that one short statement "says it all" and brings forth some emotion. Let that be okay. See if you can write through this emotion to a place of forgiveness, acceptance, and even loving. Remember, we are all doing the best we can with what we have. So are they.

4. DAILY AFFIRMATIONS AND APPRECIATIONS:

Each morning write down a positive thought in a small journal to guide you through your day. In addition, write at least three appreciations of yourself about qualities, abilities, or things which you have done well from the previous day. Done on a daily basis this can be a powerful process for preventing resentful reactions to high risk students who are often very poor at saying thanks, even though they may feel it inside.

GUIDELINES FOR READING STUDENT JOURNALS

1. Confidentiality

It is important to give the students the freedom to keep their journal section relatively private if they choose. Many students look forward to teachers reading their journal work, others like to keep it strictly private, and some prefer to share portions of the journal and keep other parts private.

Allow the students to clip or tab the journal pages that they wish to keep private. Assure them that neither you nor others will look at those pages other than to glance to see that the assignment is completed. Keeping this agreement and letting them know you can be trusted in this way can allow for deeper personal sharing in the journal.

2. Essentially, there are five general types of responses to student journal writing:

   1. **I UNDERSTAND.** *("I hear you." "It happened to me." "Are you saying that . . . .")*
   2. **YOU CAN DO IT.** *("Go for it." "I know it seems tough, but . . . .")*
   3. **YOU ARE VALUABLE.** *("I am impressed with your . . . ." "What a guy!")*
   4. **I AM AVAILABLE TO YOU.** *("Why don't you see me about this?")*
   5. **I CARE ABOUT YOU.** *("I am really touched by . . . ." "You caught my heart.")*

SUGGESTIONS

Read the journals only during quiet uninterrupted time. You may want to play relaxing music and make your external and internal environments as peaceful and nurturing as possible.

STUDENT SAMPLES

(WITH TEACHER'S COMMENT)

AN IMPORTANT EVENT IN MY LIFE:

My Dad's death changed my life a lot because I knew I was not going to have any fun times at the Lincoln Park playing soccer with my dad or running around the hill. No more going to the beach and fishing. No more nice restaurants early on Sunday mornings, and no more garage sales. It's like as if someone cut off my wings, and I was going to rot, if I didn't get out more often.

A very sad time.

Then my Mom said, "We're moving," and that was like her shooting in my face with my hands tied behind my back, because I had everything; well almost everything, I wanted and the thought of moving from my place - I felt I couldn't take it. I ran away. Maybe I thought that by running away I would make her change her mind. And the strangest thing happened to me on my way to my Grandmother's house, which is where I ran to. I kept seeing my Dad's face on at least five men on my way from East L.A. to West L.A. (2 buses needed). And I remembered that my Mom had told me once that my Dad ran away at the age of 13. I was 12 when I ran away.

The thing that radically changed my life was my Dad's death, because our home lost its order. I still can't let it go, for I dream of that place frequently.

Perhaps you can create a place like this in your heart and later in your life with your own family.

LETTER TO MOM

Mom, every time you had problems you would call Josie to help you solve them, and if I even gave my opinion you would send me to the bathroom, and that hurt because I was sent there more than nine times.

A lot of hurt here.

But then again I was a bit too small to know what I was saying, and I know you were too tired to listen to a kid that really didn't think about the seriousness of your problems.

Why did you make me leave my place? I loved it there and you didn't stop to think about that. But since I'm young I still can return someday. And the only reason you wanted us to move was that your parents also did the same to you and you wanted to return to your place. And I am now grateful for I met people that hurt me and also met people that seemed to want to help me.

That's how I feel.

I am glad you are here.

HOW I FIX MYSELF IN THE MORNING

I regularly wake up at 5:30 a.m., take a shower, untangle my hair, eat, brush my teeth, put moisturizer on, dress, fix my face, put on acne mask, mascara, lipstick, and finish off with some powder. I try to comb my hair the way I want it. Clean up the place enough so it would be presentable, pack my purse with pens, liquid paper, make-up needs and I.D.'s.

What a job!

Then I gather my books and put the keys in my purse.

On my way out I put on some perfume and jewelry. As I go down the stairs I wonder if I look a little bit pretty, or if I look ridiculous.

STUDENT JOURNAL

PART 1

REFLECTIONS

Reflections is a place in your journal for you to be with yourself, and express how you are feeling and what you are thinking. These are your private thoughts that you will not need to share with anyone. You get to write about whatever is going on with yourself, your family, your friends, at school, at home, at work, etc. Feel free to express your highs, lows, things you're upset or concerned about, or things about which you are happy and excited. There is no need to impress anyone or even yourself here. Reflections is for you.

Use this section often, daily or several times a week - for at least five or ten minutes at a time. You can use a different page each day or write many days' worth on the same page. Enjoy your time with yourself.

Date: _____

REFLECTIONS

Date: _____

REFLECTIONS

Date: _____

REFLECTIONS

Date: _____

REFLECTIONS

Date: _____

HONESTY WHEEL

Often events, situations, and the ways you react and feel about what's going on happen quickly. Feelings may come on so strongly without your always knowing why. Matching your feelings with your thoughts and your actions often allows for clearer understanding.

The Honesty Wheel gives you a chance to "catch" your feelings and discover what they are about and how to direct them for your best interest. Honesty is being aware of what is really going on with you at any present time. It could be that you are nervous, worried, or relaxed. Honesty is being open to being "real" with where you are.

STEPS

1. Turn to the Honesty Wheel activity sheet. In the inner circle, write your name.

2. In the outer circle, write several words that describe how you are feeling right now (i.e., happy, tired, confident, embarrassed, excited, upset, angry, shy, humorous, etc.)

3. Then choose one or two of the words and alongside the circles expand that word into a couple of sentences.

   Example:

   I feel angry because some kids in the hallway made some rude remarks about me.
   I feel confused because I don't know whether or not to confront them about it.

4. Next, in the middle circle, write several of your positive qualities, even if you are not feeling that way right now. (If you have already written some positive qualities in the outside circle, write some more in the middle circle. Remember that even though your honest feelings change from hour to hour (and even minute to minute), you can choose to know that, in fact, you are always a terrific and worthwhile person. You truly are a great person even if you forget or don't feel that way.

5. Then choose one or two of these words and expand that word into a couple of sentences.

   Example:

   I am honest because it's okay for me to accept my different feelings.
   I am kind because I help my parents with chores around the home.

HONESTY WHEEL

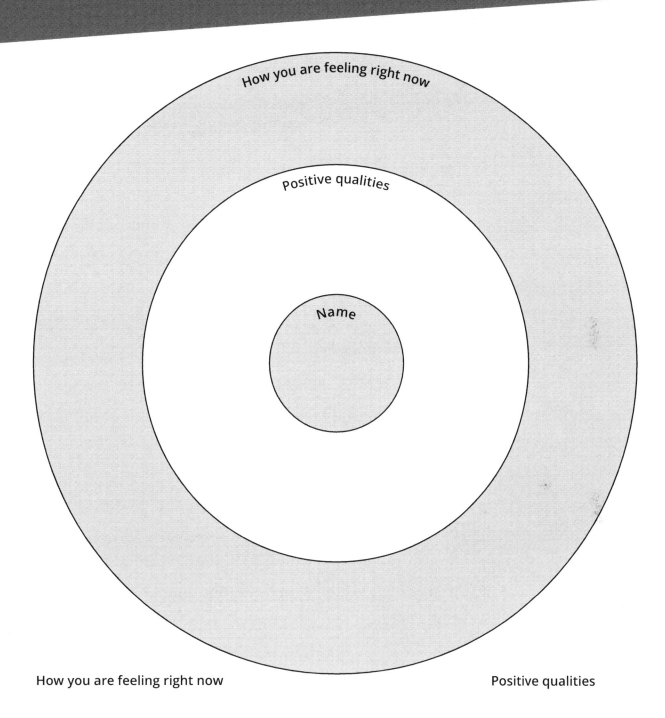

How you are feeling right now

Positive qualities

MAKING THE BEST OF ME | CHAPTER 7: VII-17

HONESTY WHEEL (EXAMPLE)

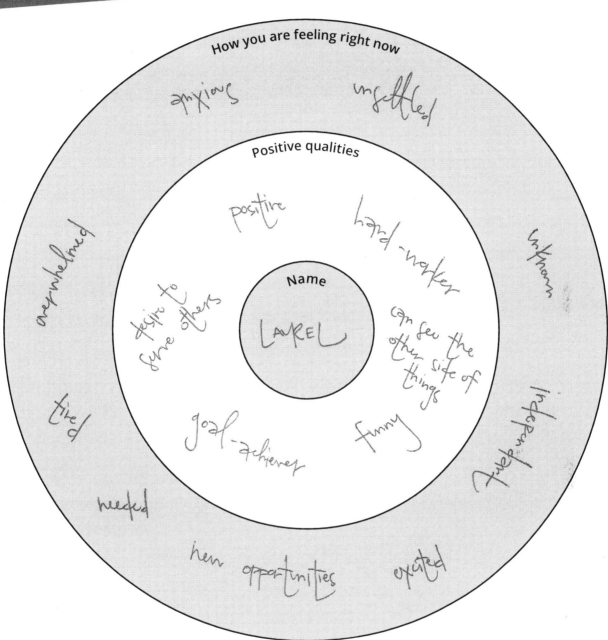

How you are feeling right now

- I feel overwhelmed because I just moved and there is still so much that needs to be done and it doesn't seem like there is an end in sight.
- I feel needed because I babysit my sister's kids when she is busy with work.

Positive qualities

- I am positive because I always look at the good that comes from trials.
- I am a hard-worker because it feels good and worthwhile to get things accomplished.

MAKING THE BEST OF ME | CHAPTER 7: VII-19

LOOKING BACK OVER MY WEEK

Towards the end of each week, spend several minutes to review in your mind the week—what happened and how you were throughout the week. Let yourself look back over the high spots and low points and what you may have learned about yourself. Then take a few minutes to complete this review:

Week of _____.

This week I appreciate myself for:

1.

2.

3.

This week I forgive myself for judging myself for:

1.

2.

3.

I am a winner! My successes this week were:

1.

2.

3.

STUDENT JOURNAL

PART 2

TOPICS

1. An important event in my life. Tell about an event that was really important and changed your life a lot.

2. Describe your same sex parent and tell how he or she is similar to you and how he or she is different from you. (If you don't know your same sex parent, use the adult of your sex who is closest to you.)

3. Things in this world that touch my heart.

4. A love letter - Write a letter to someone you love or loved, like an ex-boyfriend or girlfriend, or the boyfriend or girlfriend of your dreams. Know that you do not have to deliver this letter. First, tell them something about how you are and how you are feeling. Tell them something personal about yourself. Second, tell them something positive you notice about them. Then tell them something that shows you understand them. Then, in your own words, show them your love for them.

5. Write a list of 20 good things about yourself.

6. Pick a popular fairy tale and write the story of your life as a fairy tale.

7. If the world is going to end and you are going to go to the only island left with three people, which three people in your life would you choose to take with you to live with and why.

8. Something I did when I was little that got me in trouble.

9. A letter of encouragement to that little kid in number 8.

10. Something that happened to me when I was little that frightened me.

11. A letter to the kid in number 10 telling him that you will be his/her friend and that you will be there to protect him/her when he/she needs it.

12. If I were an animal, which animal would I choose to be and why.

13. If I could make myself invisible, what would I do.

14. (After a visit to a Convalescent Hospital) What were your thoughts and feelings as you were at the hospital? How do you feel about growing old?

15. How I fix myself up in the morning to go to school and what I think about.

16. If I had an accident and was paralyzed from the waist down, what would I do?

17. If the same thing in number 16 happened to my boyfriend or girlfriend, what would I do?

Do 18 through 21 for either parents or stepparents whether they live with you or not:

18. Letter to your mom (not to be delivered) telling her all the things that you have resented or held against her. Then tell her that you forgive her.

19. Letter to your mom (not to be delivered) telling her all the things you appreciate about her.

20. Letter to your dad (not to be delivered) telling him all the things that you have resented or held against him. Then tell him that you forgive him.

21. Letter to your dad (not to be delivered) telling him all the things that you appreciate about him.

22. A letter to yourself forgiving yourself for all the judgments (one by one) you held against your mom or your dad.

23. A favorite place I like to be by myself.

24. Create a private room for special talks; a magical room, where you can find miracles. Describe the room. Make it a really beautiful and comfortable room located in some beautiful location.

25. Imagine that you have a magic wand and call into your room whomever you want. Now invite in various people and describe your talk with them (i.e., movie stars, loved ones who have passed away, or people you want to become closer with.)

26. Tell about an incident where you demonstrated courage...you took a considerable risk and were successful.

27. Choose five people, tell what animal they remind you of and why.

28. Describe the perfect graduation dress/suit.

29. Describe the perfect date, the guy or girl, the car, where you go, what you do.

30. If you had to exchange your life for one day with someone, who would you choose and what would you do that day.

31. If you could, how would you change your appearance. Shape of face, eyes, nose, figure, size, hair, muscles, clothes, teeth, etc.

32. After the assignment above, write about your best physical features. Don't be shy. What do you think is pretty good about the way you look.

APPENDIXES

EDUCARE AT A GLANCE

Established in 1990, the EduCare Foundation is a 501(c)(3) educational organization providing high quality afterschool enrichment and student success programs to low-income youth. EduCare's nationally recognized programs have resulted in preventing destructive social behaviors such as substance abuse, violence, and crime, while promoting healthy relationships in the home, at school, and in the community. Since its inception, EduCare has served over 230,000 students, as well as provided professional development to 36,000 teachers and parents across 425 schools, both locally and nationally.

EDUCARE'S IMPACT

Over 30,000 students participate annually in **EduCare's Afterschool Programs.**

EduCare ACE Program participants are 11.4% more likely to meet or exceed standards in math than participants in the general afterschool program and 19.3% more likely to do so than non-afterschool program participants.

EduCare provides 108 middle and high schools with **EduCare Student Support Services.**

EduCare Afterschool Program participants graduate at a 21–30% higher rate than non-participants.

> "Inspiring and empowering young people to become responsible citizens, compassionate leaders, and to live their dreams."
>
> – EduCare Foundation Mission Statement

EDUCARE'S PROGRAMS

AFTERSCHOOL PROGRAMS

Provided daily at 19 LAUSD high schools, two LAUSD middle schools, one Green Dot high school, and two Lynwood high schools. Offers students opportunities to develop unique abilities, build relationships, and find relevance in educational experience.

ACE (ACHIEVEMENT AND COMMITMENT TO EXCELLENCE)

Our flagship program empowers students to achieve excellence in social, personal, and academic pursuits. Firmly rooted in Heartset® Education.

ACE INITIATIVE

Currently in three schools, the Initiative – a practical outgrowth of ACE – weaves Heartset® Education into a school's culture, developing learning communities of kindness. Provides on-site staff and year-round ACE workshops and support for students, educators and parents.

HEARTSET® EDUCATOR INSTITUTE AND HEARTSET® EDUCATION CERTIFICATION COURSE

Provides school leaders, teachers, and afterschool practitioners with practical skills for developing successful learning environments infused with proven social-emotional learning (SEL) practices.

Throughout the year, EduCare also offers **Professional Development, Parent and Family Skills Workshops** *and* **Specialized Student Services** *including English Language Learning, STEM, Healthy Choices, and Service Leadership.*

EDUCARE'S RECOGNITION

EduCare After School Programs recognized as A Best Practice / Dropout Prevention Afterschool Alliance (D.C., 2012)

David Chow Humanitarian Award Awarded to Stu Semigran, EduCare's President and Co-Founder, for work in education and serving youth (2012)

ACE Program cited in Temescal Associates' report, "Promising Activities, Practices, and Resources Promoting SEL and Character Skills in Expanded Learning Programs" (2018)

EDUCARE FOUNDATION
16134 Wyandotte St.
Van Nuys, CA 91406
818.646.5220
www.educarefoundation.com
info@educarefoundation.com

BIBLIOGRAPHY

Canfield, Jack and Wells, Harold, C. **100 Ways to Enhance Self-Concept in the Classroom: A Handbook for Teachers and Parents.** Englewood Cliffs, NJ: Prentice-Hall, 1976.

Carnevale, Anthony P., et.al. **Workplace Basics: The Skills Employers Want.** U.S. Dept. of Labor, Employment & Training Administration.

Carroll, Kathleen, Lyne, Sandy, and Blythe, Sandy. **Quest Book.**

Durfee, Cliff. **More Teachable Moments.** San Diego: Live, Love Laugh Publishing, 1983.

Gawain, Shatki. **Creative Visualization.** Berkeley, CA: Whatever Publishing, 1978.

Gibbs, Jeanne. **Tribes: A Process for Social Development and Cooperative Learning.** Santa Rosa, CA: Center Source Publications, 1987.

Hawley, Robert C. and Hawley, Isabel L. **Building Motivation in the Classroom.** Amherst, MA.: ERA Press, 1979.

Helmsteller, Shad. **What To Say When You Talk To Yourself.** Scottsdale, AZ: Grindle Press, 1986.

Hoper, Claus, et al. **Awareness Games.** New York: St. Martin's Press, 1975.

Insight Consulting Group. **Managing Accelerated Productivity: Study Guide.** Santa Monica, CA : Insight Publishing, 1987.

Jacobs, Marjorie, et al. **Building a Positive Self-Concept.** Portland, ME: J. Weston Walch, Publishing, 1988.

John-Roger and McWilliams, Peter. **You Can't Afford The Luxury Of A Negative Thought**. Los Angeles: Prelude Press, 1988.

New Games Foundation. **The New Games Book.** Garden City, NY: Doubleday/Dolphin Books, 1976.

O'Halloran, Alec. **Owner's Manual of the Personal Achievement Kit.** Sydney, N.S.W., Australia: Alec O'Halloran, Publisher, 1985.

Olney, Claude W. **Where There's A Will There's An "A".** Paoli, PA: Chesterbrook Educational Publishers, 1989.

Ostrander, Sheila, and Schroeder, Lynn. **Superlearning.** New York: Dell Publishing, 1979.

Peake, Patric. **The Principles of Positive Growth.** Calexico, CA

Peake, Patric. **'We Miss You, Alicia!' (Recognizing, Regarding and Retrieving the Ultimate Drop-Out).** Calexico, CA

Project S.E.L.F., L.A Unified School District, 1980.

Reasoner, Robert W. **Building Self-Esteem: Teacher's Guide and Classroom Materials.** Palo Alto, CA: Consulting Psychologists Press, 1986.

Rich, Dorothy. **Megaskills.** Boston: Houghton Mifflin, 1988.

Richmond, Margaret and Burge, Kathyrn. **Life Skills.** Sydney, N.S.W., Australia: Life Skills Pty. 1981.

Robbins, Anthony. **Unlimited Power.** New York: Ballantine Books, 1986.

Semigran, Candy. **One-Minute Self-Esteem: The Gift of Giving.** Santa Monica, CA: Insight Publishing, 1988.

Semigran, Candy. **250 Ways to Enhance Your Self-Esteem.** Santa Monica, CA: Insight Publishing, 1988.

Simon, Sidney, Howe, Leland W., and Kirshenbaum, Howard. **Values Clarification: A Handbook of Practical Strategies for Teachers and Students.** New York: Hart Publishing, 1972.

Tice, Louis. **Achieving Your Potential: A Family Series.** Seattle, WA: The Pacific Institute, 1979.

Weinstein, Matt and Goodman, Joel. **Playfair.** San Luis Obispo, CA: Impact Publishers, 1980.

ACTIVITIES CALENDAR

SEPTEMBER

I-04	Friendship Pie
I-06	Autobiographical Sketch
I-12	Match Up Game
I-14	Cooperative Games
I-20	Class Contract
I-24	Getting to Know Someone
I-26	Meet Someone Unique
I-29	Photo Search
I-30	Free Advice
I-34	Grab Bag
I-36	Speaking Out
II-04	Appreciation
II-06	Be a Friend to Yourself
II-08	Positive Qualities
II-40	Advertising Me
VII-11	Student Journal Part 1: Reflections
VII-20	Student Journal Part 1: Looking Back Over My Week

OCTOBER

I-22	Landmarks in my Life
I-27	Map Autobiography
I-26	Learning Chain
I-31	Mystery Person
I-32	If You Only Knew
I-33	Secret Buddy
I-35	Hot Seat
I-38	Castles in the Class
I-39	Great Person of the Year
II-10	Good News
II-12	Bragging
II-14	Unstructured Writing
IV-26	Are Your Feelings Driving You?
IV-47	Can I Quote You on That?
VI-04	Family Positions Everyone!
VI-05	Family Dynamics
VII-16	Student Journal Part 1: Honesty Wheel
VII-22	Student Journal Part 2

NOVEMBER–DECEMBER

II-16	Admiration Mirror
II-18	Self-Talk
II-22	Putdowns
II-24	Letting Go
II-28	Keeping Track of Negative Self-Talk
II-31	Practicing Positive Self-Talk
II-32	Self-Forgiveness
II-36	Affirmations
II-40	Student Affirmation
II-46	I Am Grateful For
II-48	Gratitude
II-50	Super Me Cape
III-30	Trust Circles
III-48	Making a Difference in Someone's Life
IV-38	Risk Exercise
V-56	Daily Goals
V-72	The Week in Review - 1
VI-06	Heart to Heart
VI-12	What If I Were a Parent?

JANUARY

II-34	Positive Feedback Cards
III-04	Making Friends
III-06	Power of Friendships
III-10	Friendship
III-12	What's My Feeling?
III-13	Keeping Friends
III-14	Trusting
III-16	The Ties That Bind
III-18	Team Tale
III-20	Telephone
III-22	I'm Listening
III-44	Survival
V-20	Creating the New Year
V-58	Weekly Planner
V-76	The Week in Review - 2
VI-08	Appreciation Letter

FEBRUARY

II-35	Acknowledgment
II-52	Letter to Yourself
III-24	What I Heard You Say Was...
III-26	Point of View
III-28	Talking It Out: Resolving Conflict
III-32	Expressing Resentments and Appreciations
III-34	Heart-Seat
III-35	Brainstorming
III-38	Tell it to the Teacher
III-39	Button Pushing
III-40	Forgiving
III-42	Coaching Partners
IV-04	Caring for Yourself
IV-06	Taking Care of Yourself and Helping Others
VI-10	Strength Circles
VI-18	Connecting with Family: Activities

MARCH

IV-08	Games People Play
IV-10	Examining Attitudes
IV-14	Have To/Choose To
IV-16	Impossible? Maybe Not!
IV-18	Changing Attitudes
IV-22	Learning from Mistakes
IV-24	Mock Argument
IV-30	Letting Go of Judgment and Guilt
IV-34	Letting Go of Resentment
IV-40	I Scare Myself
IV-42	Meet the Press
IV-44	Take a Stand
IV-46	I Agree/I Disagree
IV-48	Viewpoints in the Round
V-40	Creative Visualization
VI-14	Family Talk
VI-20	"Make My Day"

APRIL

II-44	Come On Down
IV-50	Broken Agreements
IV-54	Taking Charge
V-04	Getting What You Want
V-06	A New Reality
V-10	Why Go to School Anyway?
V-14	Dreaming
V-18	King/Queen of the World
V-26	The Successes of My Life
V-28	From Limitation Into Expansion
V-32	The Data Dump
VI-16	Letter of Acknowledgment
VI-22	Keys to Happiness
VI-24	What Can I Give?

MAY–JUNE

II-54	Super Booster
V-34	Cycle of Action
V-38	Magnificence
V-44	Ideal Scene
V-46	Mind Mapping
V-48	Goal Setting - Part 1 (Guidelines)
V-52	Goal Setting - Part 2 (Action Plan)
V-62	Six Steps to Achieving Excellence
V-66	Managing Money
V-70	Treasure Maps
VI-26	Making a Difference: Service

INDEX (ALPHABETICAL BY ACTIVITY)

A
V-06	A New Reality
II-33	Acknowledgment
II-16	Admiration Mirror
II-40	Advertising Me
II-34	Affirmations
II-04	Appreciation
VI-08	Appreciation Letter
IV-26	Are Your Feelings Driving You?
I-06	Autobiographical Sketch

B
II-06	Be a Friend to Yourself
I-16	Birthday Party
II-12	Bragging
III-35	Brainstorming
IV-50	Broken Agreements
III-39	Button Pushing

C
IV-47	Can I Quote You on That?
IV-04	Caring for Yourself
I-38	Castles in the Class
IV-18	Changing Attitudes
I-20	Class Contract
I-15	Clump
III-42	Coaching Partners
II-42	Come On Down
VI-18	Connecting with Family: Activities
I-14	Cooperative Games
V-20	Creating the New Year
V-40	Creative Visualization
V-34	Cycle of Action

D
V-56	Daily Goals
V-14	Dreaming

E
IV-10	Examining Attitudes
III-32	Expressing Resentments and Appreciations

F
VI-05	Family Dynamics
VI-04	Family Positions Everyone!
VI-14	Family Talk
III-40	Forgiving
I-30	Free Advice
III-10	Friendship
I-04	Friendship Pie
V-28	From Limitation Into Expansion

G
IV-08	Games People Play
I-24	Getting to Know Someone
V-04	Getting What You Want
V-48	Goal Setting - Part 1 (Guidelines)
V-52	Goal Setting - Part 2 (Action Plan)
II-10	Good News
I-34	Grab Bag
II-46	Gratitude
I-39	Great Person of the Year
VII-08	Guidelines for Reading Student Journals

H
I-17	Hand Squeeze
IV-14	Have To/Choose To
VI-06	Heart to Heart
III-34	Heart-Seat
VII-16	Honesty Wheel
I-35	Hot Seat

I
IV-46	I Agree/I Disagree
II-44	I Am Grateful For
IV-40	I Scare Myself
III-22	I'm Listening
V-44	Ideal Scene
I-32	If You Only Knew
IV-16	Impossible? Maybe Not!

K
III-13	Keeping Friends
II-26	Keeping Track of Negative Self-Talk
VI-22	Keys to Happiness
I-19	Giving & Receiving
V-18	King/Queen of the World
I-17	Knots

L

I-22	Landmarks in my Life
I-28	Learning Chain
IV-22	Learning from Mistakes
VI-16	Letter of Acknowledgment
II-50	Letter to Yourself
II-22	Letting Go
IV-30	Letting Go of Judgment and Guilt
IV-34	Letting Go of Resentment
VII-20	Looking Back Over My Week

M

V-38	Magnificence
VI-20	"Make My Day"
III-48	Making a Difference in Someone's Life
VI-26	Making a Difference: Service
III-04	Making Friends
V-66	Managing Money
I-27	Map Autobiography
I-12	Match Up Game
I-26	Meet Someone Unique
IV-42	Meet the Press
V-46	Mind Mapping
IV-24	Mock Argument
I-31	Mystery Person

N

I-15	Name Games

P

I-29	Photo Search
III-26	Point of View
II-32	Positive Feedback Cards
II-08	Positive Qualities
III-06	Power of Friendships
II-27	Practicing Positive Self-Talk
II-20	Putdowns

R

VII-11	Reflections
IV-38	Risk Exercise

S

I-33	Secret Buddy
II-30	Self-Forgiveness
II-18	Self-Talk
I-18	Sharing Circle
V-62	Six Steps to Achieving Excellence
I-36	Speaking Out
VI-10	Strength Circles
II-38	Student Affirmation
VII-10	Student Journal Part 1
VII-22	Student Journal Part 2
II-52	Super Booster
II-48	Super Me Cape
III-44	Survival

T

IV-44	Take a Stand
IV-06	Taking Care of Yourself and Helping Others
IV-54	Taking Charge
III-28	Talking It Out: Resolving Conflict
VII-04	Teacher Journal Preparation
VII-06	Teacher Journal Work
III-18	Team Tale
III-20	Telephone
III-38	Tell it to the Teacher
V-32	The Data Dump
V-26	The Successes of My Life
III-16	The Ties That Bind
V-72	The Week in Review - 1
V-76	The Week in Review - 2
I-18	Tiger, Eagle, Loving Person
V-70	Treasure Maps
III-30	Trust Circles
III-14	Trusting

U

II-14	Unstructured Writing

V

IV-48	Viewpoints in the Round

W

V-58	Weekly Planner
VI-24	What Can I Give?
III-24	What I Heard You Say Was...
VI-12	What If I Were a Parent?
III-12	What's My Feeling?
V-10	Why Go to School Anyway?

ABOUT THE AUTHORS

STU SEMIGRAN has more than forty years' experience as an educator, developing and facilitating training programs for youth and adults in educational settings worldwide. As Co-Founder and President of the EduCare Foundation and creator of EduCare's Achievement and Commitment to Excellence (ACE) Program, Stu has trained thousands of professionals, youth, educators, and parents in leadership development, afterschool & expanded learning programs, and social-emotional learning.

Since 1990, EduCare has served over 250,000 students and 40,000 teachers & parents across more than 450 schools. Stu has developed SEL/life skills curriculum, including "Making the Best of Me: A Handbook for Student Excellence and Self-Esteem," which is used in schools worldwide. He initiated EduCare's Heartset® Education model that guides educators in building kinder and more compassionate classrooms and schools.

A highly skilled and motivating speaker with an exceptional rapport with people of all ages, Stu has appeared on radio and television, and has provided training throughout the United States, Canada, Latin America, Europe, Australia, the Caribbean, Africa, and the Middle East. His presentations have included the Points of Light National Community Service Conference, National Middle School Association Annual Conference, National Association of Secondary School Principals, the National Dropout Prevention Conference, How Kids Learn Foundation, and BOOST Afterschool Conferences.

Stu currently serves on the CA Department of Education's Social and Emotional Learning (SEL) State Workgroup and LAUSD's Beyond the Bell's "Take Action Campaign" Steering Committee. In 2012, Stu was recognized as a David Chow Humanitarian Award Foundation recipient for his service to youth.

STU@EDUCAREFOUNDATION.COM • WWW.EDUCAREFOUNDATION.COM

SINDY WILKINSON, M.Ed, LMFT specializes in helping youth and teens overcome learning, attention, emotional and behavioral difficulties. With compassion, intuition, intelligence and humor, she effectively helps youth learn easier, reduce stress and be happier, while assisting their families to live together in harmony.

Sindy has over 40 years of experience in education, counseling, neurodevelopmental therapy and coaching. She holds a CA Teaching Credential and has taught children from early elementary through high school as well as undergraduate students at the University level. She has facilitated workshops for youth and adults throughout the US and in the UK. For 28 years she has enjoyed a prospering practice in marriage and family therapy including supporting at risk youth/teens as a therapist for clinics within the Alameda County, CA Behavioral Health Care System. Sindy is a Certified HANDLE Practitioner, Instructor and Supervisor. Combining her counseling, education experience and expertise, Sindy helps individuals increase self-esteem, improve relationships and move toward success. In additions to co-authoring Making the Best of Me, she developed Be UnBullyable, a curriculum for High School instructors to help their students experience the power of building strength and resilience from the inside out.

Sindy lives in the San Francisco Bay Area and is the Director of Enhanced Learning &Growth Center in Walnut Creek, CA. She loves to spend time with her daughters, read, dance, take long walks in nature, meditate, laugh, spend time with family and friends, learn new things and be by the beach whenever possible.

SINDY@LEARNINGANDGROWTH.COM • WWW.LEARNINGANDGROWTH.COM

Our vision is that love is the foundation of education.

This book is dedicated to young people everywhere who inspire us each day and are opening the way to a world of greater love and understanding.